PYTHON MACHINE LEARNING:
LEARNING:

PROGRAMMING AND DEEP LEARNING FOR BEGINNERS

THE CRASH COURSE FOR PYTHON PROGRAMMING, NEURAL NETWORKS, ARTIFICIAL INTELLIGENCE AND DATA SCIENCE

By Leonard Smith

Disclaimer

The content of this book has been checked and compiled with great care. For the completeness, correctness and topicality of the contents however no guarantee or guarantee can be taken over. The content of this book represents the personal experience and opinion of the author and is for entertainment purposes only. The content should not be confused with medical help. There will be no legal responsibility or liability for damages resulting from counterproductive exercise or errors by the reader. No guarantee can be given for success. The author therefore assumes no responsibility for the non-achievement of the goals described in the book.

Table of Contents

THE EVOLUTION OF PYTHON LANGUAGE OVER THE YEARS. 1

WHY IS PYTHON HERE TO STAY?...5

ARTIFICIAL INTELLIGENCE AND MACHINE LEARNING BASICS...11

WHY PYTHON PROGRAMMING LANGUAGE IS CONSIDERED BETTER THAN OTHER LANGUAGES 17

HOW PYTHON WORKS..22

Basic Concepts - Suitable for Beginners Level 22

Variables, types and operators 22

0- Variable names 22

1- Type int(integer: integers)...23

2- Type float (floating point numbers).....................................25

3- The type str(string: string)..27

4- The type list(list)..32

5- The type bool(boolean) 34

6- The type dict(dictionary)..36

7- Other types 37

8- Object Oriented Programming (OOP) 37

Control of the flow of instructions 40

Conditions 40

The instruction if..40

The instruction else 41

The instruction elif...43

Buckles 45

The instruction while 45

The instruction for 47

The break instruction 50

The functions 51

Interest of the functions 51

The def instruction...52

Syntax 52

Example 52

Scripts **53**

Basic Data structures **54**

The lists **54**

How to use lists as stacks 55

How to use lists as queues 56

Functional programming tools 57

Self-defined lists 58

The ruling of the **59**

Tuples and sequences **60**

Sets **62**

Dictionaries **62**

Techniques for looping **64**

More about the conditions **66**

Comparison between sequences and other types **67**

Functions **68**

Interest of the functions 68

The instruction def 69

Scope of variables: global and local variables 75

Appendix: understanding of lists 77

Classes and Modules **78**

Definition of a class 78

Importing a user-defined module 87

Class Modules, Function Modules 88

Iterators **91**

Iterators and sequences **92**

Iterators and sets **101**

Iterators and mappings **104**

Advanced Concepts - Suitable for Intermediate Level **107**

Generators: What They Are And What Problems They Solve **107**

Decorators **109**

Classes and Objects **120**

Python Math Library 124

Special Constants 125

Exponents and Logarithms 126

Arithmetic Functions 131

Trigonometric Functions 134

Type Conversion 135

Conclusion 136

Regular Expressions In Python 137

Examples of Regular Expressions 137

Data structures 142

Python Lists Vs Array Module as Arrays 143

How to create arrays? 143

How to slice arrays? 145

How to change or add elements? 146

How to remove/delete elements? 147

When to use arrays? 147

Stacks And Queues In Python 148

How do they Work? 148

Stacks and Queues using Lists 150

Stricter Implementations in Python 154

Conclusion 158

REASONS FOR LEARNING PYTHON 159

Looking at a Python Vs PHP From Another Angle 161

Python Web Frameworks To Learn In 2019 163

HOW TO SHAPE YOUR FUTURE WITH DATA SCIENCE 168

How data science can change your future 170

THE FUTURE IS NOW: MACHINE LEARNING HAS ARRIVED 172

Machine Learning Python: the language of the business of the future

.. 173

Conclusion 175

Appreciation 176

THE EVOLUTION OF PYTHON LANGUAGE OVER THE YEARS

According to several websites, Python is one of the most popular coding languages of 2015. Along with being a high-level and general-purpose programming language, Python is also object-oriented and open source. At the same time, a good number of developers across the world have been making use of Python to create GUI applications, websites and mobile apps. The differentiating factor that Python brings to the table is that it enables programmers to flesh out concepts by writing less and readable code. The developers can further take advantage of several Python frameworks to mitigate the time and effort required for building large and complex software applications.

The programming language is currently being used by a number of high-traffic websites including Google, Yahoo Groups, Yahoo Maps, Linux Weekly News, Shopzilla and Web Therapy. Likewise, Python also finds great use for creating gaming, financial, scientific and educational applications. However, developers still use different versions of the programming language. According to the usage statistics and market share data of Python posted on W3techs, currently Python 2 is being used by 99.4% of websites, whereas Python 3 is being used only by 0.6% of websites. That is why, it becomes essential for each programmer to understand different versions of Python, and its evolution over many years.

How Python Has Been Evolving over the Years?

Conceived as a Hobby Programming Project

Despite being one of the most popular coding languages of 2015, Python was originally conceived by Guido van Rossum as a hobby project in December 1989. As Van Rossum's office remained closed during Christmas, he was looking for a hobby project that will keep him occupied during the holidays. He planned to create an interpreter for a new scripting language, and named the project as Python. Thus, Python was originally designed as a successor to ABC programming language. After writing the interpreter, Van Rossum made the code public in February 1991. However, at present the open source programming language is being managed by the Python Software Foundation.

Version 1 of Python

Python 1.0 was released in January 1994. The major release included a number of new features and functional programming tools including lambda, filter, map and reduce. The version 1.4 was released with several new features like keyword arguments, built-in support for complex numbers, and a basic form of data hiding. The major release was followed by two minor releases, version 1.5 in December 1997 and version 1.6 in September 2000. The version 1 of Python lacked the features offered by popular programming languages of the time. But the initial versions created a solid foundation for development of a powerful and futuristic programming language.

Version 2 of Python

In October 2000, Python 2.0 was released with the new list comprehension feature and a garbage collection system. The syntax for the list comprehension feature was inspired by other functional programming languages like Haskell. But Python 2.0, unlike Haskell, gave preference to alphabetic keywords over punctuation characters. Also, the garbage collection system effectuated collection of reference cycles. The major release was followed by several minor releases. These releases added a number of functionality to the programming language like support for nested scopes, and unification of Python's classes and types into a single hierarchy. The Python Software Foundation has already announced that there would be no Python 2.8. However, the Foundation will provide support to version 2.7 of the programming language till 2020.

Version 3 of Python

Python 3.0 was released in December 2008. It came with a several new features and enhancements, along with a number of deprecated features. The deprecated features and backward incompatibility make version 3 of Python completely different from earlier versions. So many developers still use Python 2.6 or 2.7 to avail the features deprecated from last major release. However, the new features of Python 3 made it more modern and popular. Many developers even switched to version 3.0 of the programming language to avail these awesome features.

Python 3.0 replaced print statement with the built-in print() function, while allowing programmers to use custom separator between lines. Likewise, it simplified the rules of ordering comparison. If the operands are not organized in a natural and meaningful order, the ordering comparison operators can now raise a TypeError exception. The version 3 of the programming language further uses text and data instead of Unicode and 8-bit strings. While treating all code as Unicode by default it represents binary data as encoded Unicode.

As Python 3 is backward incompatible, the programmers cannot access features like string exceptions, old-style classes, and implicit relative imports. Also, the developers must be familiar with changes made to syntax and APIs. They can use a tool called "2to3" to migrate their application from Python 2 to 3 smoothly. The tool highlights incompatibility and areas of concern through comments and warnings. The comments help programmers to make changes to the code, and upgrade their existing applications to the latest version of programming language.

Latest Versions of Python

At present, programmers can choose either version 3.4.3 or 2.7.10 of Python. Python 2.7 enables developers to avail improved numeric handling and enhancements for standard library. The version further makes it easier for developers to migrate to Python 3. On the other hand, Python 3.4 comes with several new features and library modules, security improvements and CPython implementation improvements.

However, a number of features are deprecated in both Python API and programming language. The developers can still use Python 3.4 to avail support in the longer run.

Version 4 of Python

Python 4.0 is expected to be available in 2023 after the release of Python 3.9. It will come with features that will help programmers to switch from version 3 to 4 seamlessly. Also, as they gain experience, the expert Python developers can take advantage of a number of backward compatible features to modernize their existing applications without putting any extra time and effort. However, the developers still have to wait many years to get a clear picture of Python 4.0. However, they must monitor the latest releases to easily migrate to the version 4.0 of the popular coding language.

The version 2 and version 3 of Python are completely different from each other. So each programmer must understand the features of these distinct versions, and compare their functionality based on specific needs of the project. Also, he needs to check the version of Python that each framework supports. However, each developer must take advantage of the latest version of Python to avail new features and long-term support.

WHY IS PYTHON HERE TO STAY?

Python, like we originally mentioned, was originally conceived by Van Rossum as a hobby language in December 1989. Also, the major and backward-incompatible version of the general-purpose programming language was released on 3rd December 2008. But Python is recently rated by a number of surveyors as the most popular coding language of 2019. The massive popularity indicates Python's effectiveness as a modern programming language. At the same time, Python 3 is currently used by developers across the worlds for creating a variety of desktop GUI, web and mobile applications. There are also a number of reasons why the huge popularity and market share of Python will remain intact over a longer period of time.

8 Reasons Why the Massive Popularity of Python Will Remain Intact in the Future

1) Supports Multiple Programming Paradigms

Good developers often take advantage of different programming paradigms to reduce the amount of time and efforts required for developing large and complex applications. Like other modern programming languages, Python also supports a number of commonly used programming styles including object-oriented, functional, procedural and imperative. It further features automatic memory management, along with a dynamic type system. So programmers can use the language to effectuate development of large and complex software applications.

2) Doesn't Require Programmers to Write Lengthy Code

Python is designed with complete focus on code readability. So the programmers can create readable code base that can be used by members of distributed teams. At the same time, the simple syntax of the programming language enables them to express concepts without writing longer lines of code. The feature makes it easier for developers to large and complex applications within a stipulated amount of time. As they can easily skip certain tasks required by other programming languages, it becomes easier for developers to maintain and update their applications.

3) Provides a Comprehensive Standard Library

Python further scores over other programming languages due to its extensive standard library. The programmers can use these libraries to accomplish a variety of tasks without writing longer lines of code. Also, the standard library of Python is designed with a large number of high use programming tasks scripted into it. Thus, it helps programmers to accomplish tasks like string operations, development and implementation of web services, working with internet protocols, and handling operating system interface.

4) Effectuates Web Application Development

Python is designed as a general-purpose programming language, and lacks built-in web development features. But the web developers use a variety of add-on modules to write modern web applications in Python. While writing web applications in Python, programmers have option to use several high-level web frameworks including Django, web2py, TurboGears, CubicWeb, and Reahl. These web frameworks help programmers to perform a number of operations, without writing additional code, like database manipulation, URL routing, session storage and retrieval, and output template formatting. They can further use the web frameworks to protect the web application from cross-site scripting attacks, SQL injection, and cross-site request forgery.

5) Facilitates Development of High Quality GUI, Scientific and Numeric Applications

Python is currently available on major operating systems like Windows, Mac OS X, Linux and UNIX. So the desktop GUI applications written in the programming language can be deployed on multiple platforms. The programmers can further speedup cross-platform desktop GUI application development using frameworks like Kivy, wxPython and PyGtk. A number of reports have highlighted that Python is used widely for development of numeric and scientific applications. While writing scientific and numeric applications in Python, the developers can take advantage of tools like Scipy, Pandas, IPython, along with the Python Imaging Library.

6) Simplifies Prototyping of Applications

Nowadays, each organization wants to beat competition by developing software with distinct and innovative features. That is why; prototyping has become an integral part of modern software development lifecycle. Before writing the code, developers have to create prototype of the application to display its features and functionality to various stakeholders. As a simple and fast programming language, Python enables programmers to develop the final system without putting any extra time and effort. At the same time, the developers also have option to start developing the system directly from the prototype simply by refactoring the code.

7) Can also be used for Mobile App Development

Frameworks like Kivy also make Python usable for developing mobile apps. As a library, Kivy can be used for creating both desktop applications and mobile apps. But it allows developers to write the code once, and deploy the same code on multiple platforms. Along with interfacing with the hardware of the mobile device, Kivy also comes with built-in camera adapters, modules to render and play videos, and modules to accept user input through multi-touch and gestures. Thus, programmers can use Kivy to create different versions of the same applications for iOS, Android and Windows Phone. Also, the framework does not require developers to write longer lines of code while creating Kivy programs. After creating different versions of the mobile app, they can package the app separately for individual app store. The option makes it easier for developers to create different versions of the mobile app without deploying separate developers.

8) Open Source

Despite being rated as the most popular coding language of 2015, Python is still available as open source and free software. Along with large IT companies, the startups and freelance software developers can also use the programming language without paying any fees or royalty. Thus, Python makes it easier for businesses to reduce development cost significantly. At the same time, the programmers can also avail the assistance of large and active community to add out-of-box features to the software application.

The last major release of Python took place in December 2008. Python 3 was released as a backward-incompatible version with most of the major features back ported to Python 2.6 and 2.7. However, the programming language is being updated by the community at regular intervals. The community released Python 3.4.3 on 23rd February, 2015 with several features and patches. So the developer can always use the most recent version of the Python programming language to effectuate development of various software applications.

Why learn to program in Python

Python is an easy language and you can learn to program in Python online. It is a good starting point for your career.

Python is an interpreted programming language that arose at the beginning of the 90s thanks to its creator Guido Van Rossum and its name is due to the fondness of its developer to the British comic group Monty Python.

How to learn to program

It is not a novelty that more and more people are learning to program online and are interested in the world of development. However, many do not know where to start. And it is normal.

Nowadays there are many programming languages and platforms. If we start with a complex language without knowing the bases of programming, we may give up in our efforts, but if we start with an easy, powerful and versatile programming language that gives us the opportunity to do practically any type of application, we will be in the right path. Luckily, you can learn to program in Python online.

Schedule in Python

The digital transformation has arrived. Everyone is able to program if he tries and from now on we stop being consumers of technology to become creators.

What is the best language to start programming? Python is. It is a multi-paradigm language, which means that it combines the properties of different programming languages. It is an object-oriented language, but it is also used for imperative programming and functional programming. Best of all, you can even learn Python by playing.

In addition, it is an interpreted programming language, which means that it is not compiled as Java, but interpreted at runtime. This makes it a slower programming language when it is executed, but the truth is that it is not a problem because nowadays the difference with other programs is minimal.

Python for web development

Python is widely used for the development of web applications with Flask or Django, which are two frameworks used by many programmers. It is true that there are many frameworks to create web applications such as Laravel, but with Django you will achieve incredible results in a very short time.

Python for scripting

Throughout the years, Python has had a lot of use as a scripting tool. In fact, some of the tools used for server management and infrastructure are based on Python, such as Ansible.

Data Science, Big Data and Artificial Intelligence with Python

We already talked about the tools and programming languages essential for data analysis, and Python plays a very important role in these fields.

Artificial intelligence, big data or machine learning are fields that are still to be explored, so if you are interested in the world of data, you should learn Python. In addition, you can develop your own applications to run them in Apache Spark.

Python is a language with a great community behind that will always help you in everything you need. It is an easy language to learn and has a very clean and simple syntax. In addition, it is used by large companies such as IBM or Google and there are many job offers to be a Python programmer, so you will not go wrong learning this language.

In addition, neural nets provide the foundation for deep learning, which is a particular kind of machine learning. Deep learning uses a certain set of machine learning algorithms that run in multiple layers. It is made possible, in part, by systems that use GPUs to process a whole lot of data at once.

If you're confused by all these different terms, you're not alone. Computer scientists continue to debate their exact definitions and probably will for some time to come. And as companies continue to pour money into artificial intelligence and machine learning research, it's likely that a few more terms will arise to add even more complexity to the issues.

Introduction to Machine Learning

Machine Learning is the branch of Artificial Intelligence that aims to develop techniques that allow computers to learn. More concretely, it is about creating algorithms capable of generalizing behaviors and recognizing patterns based on information provided in the form of examples. It is, therefore, a process of induction of knowledge , that is, a method that allows to obtain by generalization a general statement from statements that describe particular cases.

When all the particular cases have been observed, the induction is considered complete, so that the generalization to which it gives rise is considered valid. Not obstinate, in most cases it is impossible to obtain a complete induction, so the statement that gives rise is subject to a certain degree of uncertainty, and therefore cannot be considered as a scheme of formally valid inference or can justify empirically. On many occasions the field of action of machine learning overlaps with that of Data Mining, since the two disciplines are focused on data analysis, however, machine learning focuses more on the study of the computational complexity of problems with the intention of making them feasible from the practical point of view, not only theoretical.

At a very basic level, we could say that one of the tasks of the AA is to try to extract knowledge about some unobserved properties of an object based on the properties that have been observed of that same object (or even of properties observed in other similar objects).) ... or, in more plain words, predict future behavior based on what has happened in the past. A very current example would be, for example, to predict if a particular product will like a customer based on the ratings that same customer has made other products that have been tested.

In any case, as the topic we are talking about is related to learning, the first thing we have to ask ourselves is: What do we mean by learning? And, since we want to give general methodologies to produce an automatic learning, once we fix this concept we will have to give methods to measure the degree of success or failure of a learning. In any case, since we are transferring an intuitive concept and that we normally use in everyday life to a computational context, it must be taken into account that all the definitions that we give of learning from a computational point of view, as well as the different forms of to measure it, they will be intimately related to very specific contexts and possibly far from what intuitively, and in a general way, we understand by learning.

A relatively general definition of learning within the human context could be the following: process through which skills, skills, knowledge, behaviors or values are acquired or modified as a result of study, experience, instruction, reasoning and observation. From this definition it is important to note that learning must occur from the experience with the environment, learning is not considered all that skill or knowledge that are innate in the individual or that are acquired as a result of the natural growth of it. Following a similar scheme, in the ML we will consider learning what the machine can learn from experience, not from the recognition of patterns programmed a priori. Therefore, a central task of how to apply this definition to the context of computing is to feed the machine experience through objects with which to train (examples) to subsequently apply the patterns that have been recognized on other objects different (in a product recommendation system, an example would be a particular customer or product pair, together with the information about the assessment that he has made of it).

There are a large number of problems that fall within what we call inductive learning. The main difference between them lies in the type of objects they try to predict. Some common classes are:

- **Regression:** They try to predict a real value. For example, predict the value of the bag tomorrow from the behavior of the bag that is stored (past). Or predict the grade of a student in the final exam based on the grades obtained in the various tasks performed during the course.
- **Classification (binary or multiclass):** They try to predict the classification of objects over a set of prefixed classes. For example, to classify if a certain news is of sports, entertainment, politics, etc. If only 2 possible classes are allowed, then it is called binary classification; if more than 2 classes are allowed, we are talking about multiclass classification .
- **Ranking:** Try to predict the optimal order of a set of objects according to a predefined relevance order. For example, the order in which a search engine returns internet resources in response to a search by a user.

Normally, when a new AA problem is addressed, the first thing that is done is to mark it within one of the previous classes, since depending on how it is classified, it will be the way in which we can measure the error committed between prediction and reality. Consequently, the problem of measuring how successful the learning obtained is should be treated for each particular case of applied methodology, although in general we can anticipate that we will need to "embed" the representation of the problem in a space in which we have defined a measure.

On the other hand, and depending on the type of output that occurs and how the treatment of the examples is addressed, the different AA algorithms can be grouped into:

- **Supervised learning:** a function is generated that establishes a correspondence between the desired inputs and outputs of the system, where the knowledge base of the system consists of examples labeled a priori (that is, examples of which we know their correct classification). An example of this type of algorithm is the classification problem we mentioned earlier.
- **Unsupervised learning:** where the modeling process is carried out on a set of examples formed only by inputs to the system, without knowing their correct classification. So it is sought that the system is able to recognize patterns to be able to label the new entries.
- **Semi supervised learning:** it is a combination of the two previous algorithms, taking into account both classified and unclassified examples.
- **Learning by reinforcement:** in this case the algorithm learns observing the world that surrounds it and with a continuous flow of information in both directions (from the world to the machine, and from the machine to the world) performing a trial-and-error process, and reinforcing those actions that receive a positive response in the world.
- **Transduction:** is similar to supervised learning, but its purpose is not to explicitly construct a function, but only to try to predict the categories in which the following examples fall based on the input examples, their respective categories and the new examples to the system . That is, it would be closer to the concept of dynamic supervised learning.
- **Multi-task learning:** encompasses all those learning methods that use knowledge previously learned by the system in order to face problems similar to those already seen.

WHY PYTHON PROGRAMMING LANGUAGE IS CONSIDERED BETTER THAN OTHER LANGUAGES

Python is a high-level scripting language. It is easy to learn and powerful than other languages because of its dynamic nature and simple syntax which allow small lines of code. Included indentation and object-oriented functional programming make it simple. Such advantages of Python makes it different from other languages and that's why Python is preferred for development in companies mostly. In industries, machine learning using python has become popular. This is because it has standard libraries which are used for scientific and numerical calculations. Also, it can be operated on Linux, Windows, Mac OS and UNIX. Students who want to make future in Python are joining online video training courses and python programming tutorial.

Features of Python

A question to arise is why machine learning using python is preferred over other languages? This is because Python has some features over other programming languages. Here are some basic features of Python making it better than other languages:

- Python is High-level language. It means the context of Python is user-friendly rather than machine language.
- The interactive nature of Python makes it simple and attractive for users. In interactive mode, users are able to check the output for each statement.
- As an Object Oriented Programming language, it allows reuse and recycling of programs.
- The syntax of Python is extensible through many libraries.

Applications of Python

There are a lot of advantages of Python making it different from others. Its applications have made it a demanded language for software development, web development, graphic designing and other use cases. Its standard libraries which support internet protocols such as HTML, JSON, XML, IMAP, FTP and many more. Libraries are able to support many operations like Data Scraping, NLP and other applications of machine learning. Due to such advantages and uses, students are preferring python programming tutorial rather than other languages. Also, there are many online video training courses available, user or any interested candidate can buy them from any place. No need to worry about location, it can be learned from their home.

How to Learn Python

Since Python has shown its enormous applications and use cases. It is mostly used in Machine Learning and Artificial intelligence companies as a basic programming language. Students who want to start their career in AI and machine learning should have a basic understanding of Python. There are many online video training courses and python programming tutorial available to join. Further, it is an easy programming language to learn as a beginner. Online courses or tutorials can help the beginners to learn Python. It can be learned quickly because user can think like a programmer due to its readable and understandable syntax. With Python we can develop anything by computer programs, only need is to spend time to understand Python and its standard libraries. PyCharm is its IDE (Integrated Development Environment) which makes interface so easy and comfortable while learning. With the help of debugging feature of PyCharm we can easily analyse the output of each line and the error can be detected easily.

Conclusion

Python is used in many big companies such as Google, Instagram, Dropbox, Reddit and many more which means more job scopes in Python. Due to increasing demand of Python programmers, students and beginners in industries are choosing Python as their core programming language. Also the features of Python make it very easy to learn. It can be concluded that Python is best language for beginners to start as well as a powerful language for development. It is good for scientific and numerical operations. Thus many students are opting online video training courses for python programming tutorial. So, they can learn from anywhere and make their career in Python programming.

How Python Is a Preferred Language for Startups?

Your business may need a dynamic web-based solution, however; the extensive range of options available in the case of programming languages may leave you confused. It is important to understand that selecting a language or a platform in a startup is definitely one of the most crucial decisions. Though there are multiple developmental languages, Python is becoming the most preferred one, especially among startups on account of multiple reasons. Apart from being renowned for its faster developmental cycles, Python can fulfill changing and increasing requirements pretty fast.

Here's a list of reasons how and why Python is a preferred language for startups:

1. User-Friendly

Python is a highly popular language mainly because of easy readability. Its uncluttered syntax helps startups use this programming language easily. Additionally, Python has an in-built dictionary data structure, which makes it user-friendly. Python also includes high-level data typing, which minimizes the length of the support code.

2. Speed and Increased Productivity

When it comes to small startups, factors like marketing speedily and new-feature implementation are of great significance. Python has an object-oriented design, which provides process control and strong integration and these lead to an increase in speed and productivity. Python is also considered as a preferable option for building complex network applications.

3. Helps Tackle Complexity

Most startups and social networks are based on the web, and Python is ideal for tackling complexity. By using Python, you can choose to overcome multiple issues such as integration of different systems, which would otherwise require more time and effort. Python also provides scalability, which is essential for startups to expand their business in the future.

4. A Small Team Suffices

Python allows programmers to document the proof about a concept easily. While using Python, a huge team of developers and designers is not required to create a premium quality product. This definitely helps startups and medium-sized organizations to save resources and try and work on various ideas.

5. Opportunity to Earn Faster

As Python helps one to work faster, with a little initial spending, startups can make larger profits. Once you build and support your project on Python, the returns come faster. Python, thus, assists startups to earn money quickly, which is definitely beneficial for them.

6. Prompt Support

Most startups prefer using Python as they get prompt support when there are serious technical issues. It also allows your product to be of high-quality and less prone to crashes.

7. Easier-to-Create Prototypes

Python is often an easy solution for large projects. It is often easier to rewrite something that is written in Python. Also, Python is useful for writing prototypes as it already has a working prototype. This feature definitely helps startups to save money and time and also see whether a business idea works or not.

In this fiercely competitive business world, it is crucial for startups to grow fast. Python helps newly formed companies get a working product in minimal time and at reduced rates.

Python does not require small businesses to hire a big team of experts. These advantages definitely make it one of the best programming languages for fledgling entities. Above points will surely clear your doubts before hiring a Python developer for your business.

HOW PYTHON WORKS

Basic Concepts - Suitable for Beginners Level

Variables, types and operators

A variable is a memory space in which it is possible to store a value (a datum).

Open   IDLE:
Start → Programs → Python → IDLE (Python GUI)

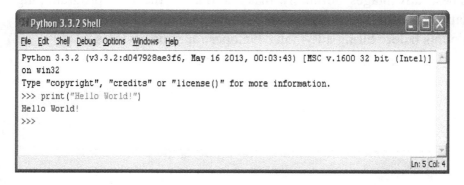

0- Variable names

The name of a variable is written with letters (not accented), numbers   or   the   underscore   _
The name of a variable must not start with a number.

In Python, the use is not to use capital letters to name the variables (they are reserved to name the classes).

Example: `age, mon_age, temperature1`

To avoid:

1- Type int(integer: integers)

To assign (we also say assign) the value 17 to the named variable age:

```
>>> age = 17
```

The function print() displays the value of the variable:

```
>>> print (age)
17
```

The function type() returns the type of the variable:

```
>>> print ( type (age))
<class 'int'>
```

int is the type of integers.

```
>>> # this is a comment
>>> age = age + 1       # plus short: age + = 1
>>> print (age)
18
>>> age = age - 3       # plus short: age - = 3
>>> print (age)
15
>>> age = age * 2                #           plus short: age * = 2
>>> print (age)
30
>>> a = 6 * 3 - 20
```

```
>>>   print (a)
-2
>>> b = 25
>>> c = a + 2 * b
>>>   print (b, c)                        # do not
forget the comma
25 48
```

The operator //gives the entire division:

```
>>> round = 450 // 360
>>>   print (round)
1
```

The operator % gives the rest of the division (modulo operation):

```
>>> angle = 450% 360
>>>   print (angle)
90
```

The operator ** gives the power:

```
>>> mo = 2 ** 20
>>>   print (mo)
1048576
>>> root2 = 2 ** 0.5
>>>   print (root2)
1.41421356237
```

2- Type float (floating point numbers)

```
>>> b = 17.0          # the decimal point is
a dot (not a comma)
>>> print (b)
 17.0
>>> print ( type (b))
 <class 'float'>
>>> c = 14.0 / 3.0
 >>> print (c)
 4.66666666667
>>> c = 14.0 // 3.0     # entire division
>>> print (c)
 4.0
```

Warning: with integers, the operator /does a classical division and returns a type float:

```
>>> c = 14/3
 >>> print (c)
 4.66666666667
```

Scientific notation:

```
>>> a = -1.784892e4
 >>> print (a)
 -17848.92
```

Mathematical functions

To use mathematical functions, you must first import the module math:

```
>>> import math
```

The function `dir()` returns the list of functions and data of a module:

```
>>> dir (math)
 ['__doc__', '__name__','package__ ','
acos', 'acosh', 'asin', 'asinh', 'atan',

'atan2', 'atanh', 'ceil', 'copysign',
'cos', 'cosh', 'degrees', 'e', 'erf',

'erfc', 'exp', 'expm1', 'fabs',
'factorial', 'floor', 'fmod', 'frexp',
'fsum',

'gamma', 'hypot', 'isinf', 'isnan',
'ldexp', 'lgamma', 'log', 'log10',
'log1p',

'modf', 'pi', 'pow', 'radians', 'sin',
'sinh', 'sqrt', 'tan', 'tanh', 'trunc']
```

To call a function of a module, the syntax is: **module.function (arguments)**

To access a data from a module: **module.data**

```
>>> print (math.pi)         # pi data of
the math module (pi number)

3.14159265359

>>> print (math.sin (math.pi / 4.0)) #
sin () function of the math module
(sinus)

0.707106781187

>> > print (math.sqrt (2.0))         #
function sqrt () of the math module
(square root)
```

1.41421356237

```
>>> print (math.sqrt (-5.0))
Traceback (most recent call last):
    print math.sqrt (-5.0)
ValueError: math domain error
>>> print (math.exp (-3.0))          # function exp () of the math module (exponential)
0.0497870683679
>>> print (math.log (math.e))     # log () function math module (natural logarithm)
1.0
```

3- The type str (string: string)

```
>>> name = 'Dupont'    #                    between apostrophes
>>> print (name)
Dupont
>>> print ( type (name))
<class 'str'>
>>> firstname = "Pierre"    # we can also use quotation marks
>>> print (first name)
Pierre
>>> print (name, first name)       #     do not forget the comma
```

```
Dupont Pierre
```

Concatenation refers to putting multiple strings together end-to-end.
Concatenation uses the operator+

```
>>> string = name + firstname     #
concatenation of two strings
>>>   print (string)

 DupontPierre
>>> string = firstname + lastname        #
concatenation of two strings
>>>   print (string)

 PierreDupont
>>> string = first name + '' + last name
 >>>   print (string)

 Pierre Dupont
>>> string = string + '18 years old'   #
plus short: string + = '18 years'
>>>   print (string)

 Pierre Dupont 18 years old
```

The function `len()` returns the length of the string:

```
>>>   print ( len (string))
 20
```

Indexing and slicing:

```
>>>   print (string [0])       #           first
character (index 0)
 P
```

```
>>>   print (string [1])          #        second
character (index 1)
i
>>>   print (string [1: 4])     # slicing
ier
>>>   print (string [2:])        # slicing
wand Dupont 18 yrs
>>>   print (string [-1])        #              last
character (subscript -1)
s
>>>   print (string [-6:])      # slicing
18 years
```

In summary :

```
+ --- + --- + --- + --- + --- + --- +
| M | u | r | i | e | l |
+ --- + --- + --- + --- + --- + --- +
 0 1 2 3 4 5 6
-6 -5 -4 -3 -2 -1
```

```
>>> string = today ' hui '
SyntaxError: invalid syntax
>>> string = 'Today \' s '          #
escape sequence \'
>>>   print (string)
```

```
 Today
>>> string = "Today" hui "
>>>  print (channel)
 Today
```

The escape sequence \n represents a line break:

```
>>> string = 'First line \ nSecond line'
>>>  print (string)
 First line
Second line
```

More simply, we can use triple quotation marks (or triple quotation marks) to enclose a string defined on several lines:

```
>>> chain = "" "First line
Second line "" "
>>>  print (string)
 First line
Second line
```

You can not mix towels and tea towels (here type str and type int):

```
>>> string = '17 .45 '
>>>  print ( type (string))
 <class' str'>
>>> string = string + 2
 TypeError: Can not convert 'int' object
to str implicitly
```

The function `float()` converts a type `str` to a type `float`

```
>>> number = float (string)
 >>>  print (number)
 17.45
>>>  print ( type (number))
 <class 'float'>
>>> number = number + 2          # plus
short: number + = 2
>>>  print (number)
 19.45
```

The function `input()` starts a command prompt (in English: prompt) to enter a string.

```
>>>  # enter a string and confirm with
the Enter key
>>> string = input ( "Enter a number:" )
 Enter a number: 14.56
 >>>  print (string)
 14.56
>>>  print ( type (string ))
 <class 'str'>
>>> number = float (string) # conversion
type
>>>  print (number ** 2)
 211.9936
```

4- The type list(list)

A list is a data structure. The first element of a list has index (index) 0. In a list, we can have elements of several types.

```
>>> infoperso = [ 'Pierre' , 'Dupont' ,
17, 1.75, 72.5]

>>>   # the infoperso list contains 5
elements of types str, str, int, float
and float

>>>  print ( type (personalinfo) )

<class 'list'>

>>>  print (personalinfo)

['Pierre', 'Dupont', 17, 1.75, 72.5]

>>>  print ( 'First Name:' , personalinfo
[0])          # first element (index 0 )

First name: Pierre

>>>   print ( 'Age:' , personalinfo [2])
             # the third element al 'index
2

Age: 17

>>>   print ('Size:' , personalinfo [3])
             # the fourth element has the
index 3

Size: 1.75
```

The function range()creates a list of regularly spaced integers:

```
>>> mylist = range (10)
 >>>   print ( list (mylist))
```

```
[0, 1, 2, 3, 4, 5, 6, 7, 8, 9]
>>> print ( type (mylist))
<class 'range'>
>>> mylist = range (1,10,2) #           range
(start, end not included, interval)
>>> print ( list (mylist))
[1, 3, 5, 7, 9]
>>> print ( malist [2])              #    the
third element has the index 2
5
```

You can create a list of lists, which is similar to a 2-dimensional array (row, column):

```
0                        1                        2
10                       11                       12
20 21 22
>>> mylist = [[0, 1, 2], [10, 11, 12],
[20, 21, 22]]
>>> print (mylist [0])
[0, 1, 2]
>>> print (mylist [0] [0])
0
>>> print (malist [2] [1])         #
element in the third line and second
column
21
>>> malist [2] [1] = 69            #    new
assignment
```

```
> >>  print (malist)
 [[0, 1, 2], [10, 11, 12], [20, 69, 22]]
```

5- The type bool (boolean)

Two values are possible: True and False

```
>>> choice = True
>>>  print ( type (choice))
 <class 'bool'>
```

Comparison operators:

Operator	Meaning	Remarks
<	strictly inferior	None
<=	less or equal	None
>	strictly superior	None
> =	greater than or equal to	None
==	equal	Caution: two signs ==
! =	different	None

```
>>> b = 10
 >>>  print (b> 8)
 True
>>>  print (b == 5)
 False
>>>  print (b! = 10)
```

```
False
>>>  print (0 <= b <= 20 )
True
```

Logical operators: `and, or, not`

```
>>> note = 13.0
>>> ab_statement = note> = 12.0 and note
<14.0 # or: ab_statement = 12.0 <= note
<14.0
>>>  print (ab_statement)
True
>>>  print ( not mention_ab)
False
>> >  print (note == 20.0 or note == 0.0)
False
```

The operator is `in` used with strings (type `str`) or lists (type `list`):

```
>>> chain = 'Good evening'
>>>  # is the 'evening' sub-chain part of
the 'Good evening' chain?
>>> result = 'soir'  in string
>>>  print (result)
True
>>>  print ( 'b'  in string)
False
>>> maliste = [4, 8, 15]
```

```
>>>   # is the integer 9 in the list?
>>>   print (9 in malist)
False
>>>   print (8 in malist)
True
>>>   print (14 not in malignant)
True
```

6- The type dict(dictionary)

A dictionary stores data in the form **key** ⇒ **value**
A key is unique and is not necessarily an integer (as is the
case with the index of a list).

```
>>> means = { 'math' : 12.5, 'english' :
15.8} # between braces
>>>   print ( type (means))
<class 'dict'>
>>>   print (averages [ 'english' ])
      # in brackets
15.8
>>> means [ 'English' ] = 14.3          #
new assignment
>>>   print (averages)
{'english': 14.3, 'math': 12.5}
>>> averages [ 'sport' ] = 11.0          #
new entry
>>>   print (averages)
```

```
{'sport': 11.0, 'English': 14.3, 'math':
12.5}
```

7- Other types

We have seen the most common types.
There are many others:

- complex (complex numbers, for example 1 + 2.5j)
- tuple (data structure)
- set (data structure)
- file

8- Object Oriented Programming (OOP)

Python is an **object-oriented** programming language (like C
++, Java, PHP, Ruby ...).
A variable is actually an **object** of a certain **class** .

For example, the variable `amis` is an object of the class
`list`.
It is also said that the variable `amis` is an **instance** of the
class `list`.
The **instantiation** (**instantiate** action) is the creation of an
object from a class (syntax: **NewObject = ClassName
(arguments)**):

```
>>>     # instantiation of the object
friends of the class list

>>> friends = [ 'Nicolas' , 'Julie' ] #
or: friends = list (['Nicolas', 'Julie'])

>>> print ( type (friends))
 <class 'list'>
```

A class has functions that we call **methods** and data that we
call **attributes** .

The `append()` class method `list` adds a new item at the
end of the list:

```
>>>   # instantiation of an empty list
>>> friends = []                    #          or:
friends = list ()
>>> friends.append ( 'Nicolas' ) #
general        synthase:        object.method
(arguments)
>>>   print (friends)
 ['Nicolas']
>>> friends.append ( 'Julie' )      #    or:
friends = friends + ['Julie']
>>>   print (friends)
 ['Nicolas', 'Julie']
> >> amis.append ( 'Pauline' )
 >>>   print (friends)
 ['Nicolas', 'Julie', 'Pauline']
>>> friends.sort ()                     #    the
sort () method sorts the elements
>>>   print (friends)
 ['Julie', 'Nicolas', 'Pauline']
>>> friends.reverse ()                  #    the
reverse () method reverses the list of
elements
>>>   print (friends)
 ['Pauline', 'Nicolas', 'Julie']
```

The method lower() of the class str returns the string in
lower case:

```
>>>   # the string variable is an instance
of the class str
>>> string = "MORNING"                    #      or:
string = str ("MORNING")
>>> string2 = string.lower ()       #      we
apply the method lower () to the string
object
>>>   print (string2)
 hello
>>>   print (string)
 HELLO
```

The pop() class method dict deletes a key:

```
>>>     # instantiation of the average
object of the class dict
>>> means = { 'sport' : 11.0, 'english' :
14.3, 'math' : 12.5}
 >>>    # or: means = dict ({' sport ':
11.0,' english ': 14.3,' math ': 12.5})
>>> medium.pop ( ' english ' )
 14.3
>>>   print (means)
 {' sport ': 11.0,' math ': 12.5}
>>>   print (averages.keys ())       #    the
keys () method returns the list of keys
dict_keys (['sport', 'math'])
```

```
>>> print (means.values ())          #    the
values () method returns the list of
values

dict_values ([11.0, 12.5])
```

Control of the flow of instructions

Conditions

The instruction if

In programming, we always need the notion of condition to allow a program to adapt to different scenarios.

Syntax.

```
if expression: # do not forget the punctuation mark ':'

    "instruction block"  # attention to the indentation (1 Tab or 4
* Spaces)

# continuation of the program
```

- If the expression is true (True) then the statement block is executed.
- If the expression is false (False), it is passed directly after the program.

Example In this example we will test whether the note entered by the user. If the note is> 10 we must receive the message: "I have the average" otherwise it will do nothing.

```
string =  input ( "Score from 20:" )

note =  float (string)

 if note > =  10.0 :

     # this block is executed if the expression (note> = 10.0) is tr
ue

    print ( "I have the mean" )
```

```
# continuation of the

print program ( "End of the program" )
```

- Code blocks are delimited by indentation.
- Indentation is mandatory in scripts.

The instruction `else`

An instruction `else`is always associated with an instruction `if`.

```
if expression:

    "statement block 1"     # attention to indentation (1 Tab or 4
* Spaces)

else :                          # else is at the same level as if

    "statement block 2"    # attention to indentation

# continued program
```

- If the expression is true (`True`) then statement block 1 is executed.
- If the expression is false (`False`) then the statement block 2 is executed.

Example In this example we will test whether the note entered by the user. If the note is> 10 we must receive the message: "I have the average" otherwise it will display "It is below average".

```
string =  input ( "Score from 20:" )

note =  float (string)

 if note > =  10.0 :

    # this block is executed if the expression (note> = 10.0) is tr
ue

    print ( "I have the mean" )
```

41

```
else :

    # this block is executed if the expression (note> = 10.0) is fa
lse

    print ( "This is below average" )

print ( "End of program" )
```

To treat the case of invalid notes (\ (<0 \) or \ (> 20 \)), we can nest conditional statements:

```
string =  input ( "Score from 20:" )

note =  float (string)

if note >  20.0  or note <  0.0 :

    # this block is executed if the expression (note> 20.0 or note
<0.0) is true

    print ( "Invalid note!" )

else :

    # this block is executed if the expression (note> 20.0 or note
<0.0) is false

    if note > =  10.0 :

        # this block is executed if the expression (note> = 10.0) i
s true

        print ( "I have the mean" )

    else :

        # this block is executed if the expression (note> = 10.0) is
false

        print ( "This is below average" )

print ( "End of the program" )
```

Or even:

```
string =  input ( "Score from 20:" )

note =  float (string)
```

42

```
if note >  20.0  or note <  0.0 :


print ( "Invalid note!" )

 else :

     if note > =  10.0 :

         print ( "I have the mean" )

         if note ==  20.0 :

             # this block is executed if the expression (note == 20.
0) is true

             print ( "That's even excellent!" )

     else :

         print ("This is below average" )

         if note ==  0.0 :

             # this block is executed if the expression (note == 0.
0) is true

             print ( "... lamentable!" )

 Print ( "End of the program " )
```

The instruction `elif`

An instruction `elif` (contraction of **else if**) is always associated with an instruction `if`.

Syntax.

```
if expression 1 :

     "instruction block 1"

elif expression 2 :

     "instruction block 2"

elif expression 3 :

     "instruction block 3"        # here two elif instructions, but the
re is no limitation
```

```
else :

    "instruction block 4"

# program continuation
```

- If the expression 1 is true then the instruction block 1 is executed, and it passes after the program.
- If the expression 1 is false then we test the expression 2:
- if the expression 2 is true, the instruction block 2 is executed, and the program is continued.
- if the expression 2 is false then we test the expression 3, etc.

The instruction block 4 is thus executed if all the expressions are false (it is the block "by default").
Sometimes there is nothing to do. In this case, the instruction can be omitted else:

```
if expression 1 :

    "instruction block 1"

elif expression 2 :

    "instruction block 2"

elif expression 3 :

    "instruction block 3"

# program continuation
```

The instruction elif often avoids the use of nested (and often complicated) conditions.

Example Several possibilities can be tested with a much cleaner syntax with the instructions if-elif-else:

```
note =  float ( input ( "Score of 20:" ))

 if note ==  0.0 :

    print ( "This is below average" )

    print ( "... lamentable!" )

 elif note ==  20.0 :
```

```
    print ( "I have the mean" )

    print ( "It's even excellent!" )

 Elif  0  < note <  10 :      # or else: elif 0.0 <note <10.0:

    print ("It's below average" )

 elif note > =  10.0  and note <  20.0 :     # or else: elif 10.0 <=
 note <20.0:

    print ( "I have the average" )

 else :

    print ( "Invalid note ! " )

 print ( " End of the program " )
```

Buckles

The instruction `while`

Syntax.

```
while expression:                # do not forget the punctuation mark ':
'

    "instruction block"   # attention to indentation (1 Tab or 4 *
Spaces)

# program continuation
```

- If the expression is true (`True`) the statement block is executed, then the expression is evaluated again.

The cycle continues until the expression is false (`False`): it then passes after the program.

Example 1: A script that counts from 1 to 4

```
# initialization of the count variable

counter =  0

while counter <  5 :
```

```
    # this block is executed as long as the condition (counter <5)
is true

    print (counter)

    counter = counter +  1      # counter increment, counter = counte
r + 1

print (counter)

 print ( "End of the loop" )
```

Example 2: Multiplication Table by 8

```
counter =  1             # initialization of the count variable

while counter <=  10 :

    # this block is executed as long as the condition (counter <= 1
0) is true

    print (counter, '* 8 =' , counter * 8 )

    counter + =  1      # incrementation of the counter, counter = co
unter + 1

print ( "Here we go!" )
```

Example 3: Displaying the current time

```
import  time      # import module time

quit =  'n'    # initialization

while quit ! =  'o' :

    # this block is executed as long as the condition is true

    # strftime () is a function of the module time

    print ( 'Current time' , time . strftime ( '% H:% M:% S' ))

    quit =  input ( "Do you want to quit the program (o / n)?" )

 print ( "See you soon" )
```

The instruction for

Syntax

```
for element in sequence:      # do not forget the punctuation mark ':
'

    "

instruction block"      # attention to the indentation (1 Tab or 4 *
  Spaces)

# continuation of the program
```

The elements of the sequence come from a string of characters or from a list.

Example with a sequence of characters

```
string =  'Goodnight'

for letter in string:      # letter is the iteration variable

    print (letter)

 print ( "End of the loop" )
```

The letter variable is initialized with the first element of the sequence ('B'). The instruction block is then executed.

Then the variable letter is updated with the second element of the sequence ('o') and the instruction block executed again ...

The instruction block is executed one last time when you arrive at the last element of the sequence ('r').

Function range()

The association with the function range()is very useful for creating automatic sequences of integers:

```
for i in  range ( 1 , 5 ):

    print (i)

 print ( "End of the loop" )
```

Example: Multiplication table

Creating a multiplication table seems easier with a loop `for`than with a loop `while`:

```
for counter in  range ( 1 , 11 ):

    print (counter, '* 8 =' , counter * 8 )

 print ( "Here we go!" )
```

Example: Calculation of a sum

For example, the expression of the following sum: $$s = \sum_{i=0}^{100} \sqrt{\frac{i \pi}{100}} \sin (\frac{i \pi}{100})$$

```
from  math  import sqrt, sin, pi

s =  0.0  # # intialisation of s

for i in  range ( 101 ):

    s + = sqrt (i * pi / 100 ) * sin (i * pi / 100 )    # equivalent
 to s = s + sqrt (x) * sin (x)

# Display of sum

print (s)
```

Exercise: Calculate (π) with the wallis **product** $$\frac{\pi}{2} = \prod_{i=1}^{p} \frac{4i^2}{4i^2-1}$$

Solution:

```
#% load wallis.py

from  math  import pi



my_pi =  1.   # intization

p =  100000

for i in  range ( 1 , p):

    my_pi * = 4 * i ** 2 / ( 4 * i ** 2 - 1. )    # implement
 ation of the Wallis formula



my_pi * = 2          # multiplication by 2 of the found value
```

```
print ( "The pi value of the library 'math':" , pi)

 print ( "The value of pi compute by the formula of Wallis:" , my_p
i)


print ( "The difference between the two values:" , abs (pi - my_pi))

 # the abs () function gives the absolute value
```

List comprehensions

List comprehensions provide a way to build lists in a very concise manner. A typical application is the construction of new lists where each element is the result of an operation applied to each element of another sequence; or to create a subsequence of elements satisfying a specific condition.

For example, suppose we want to create a list of squares, like:

```
squares = []

 for x in  range ( 10 ):

    squares . append (x ** 2 )

squares
```

Note that this creates (or replaces) a named variable xthat still exists after running the loop. We can compute a list of squares without edge effects with:

```
squares = [x ** 2  for x in  range ( 10 )]

squares
```

which is shorter and readable.

A list comprehension consists of placing in brackets an expression followed by a clause forand then by zero or more clauses foror if. The result is a new list result of the evaluation of the expression in the context of the clauses forand ifwho follow it. For example, this list comprehension combines the elements of two lists if they are not equal:

```
combs = [(x, y) for x in [ 1 , 2 , 3 ] for y in [ 3 , 1 , 4 ] if x !
= y]
```

```
combs
```

and it's equivalent to:

```
combs = []
  for x in [ 1 , 2 , 3 ]:
      for y in [ 3 , 1 , 4 ]:
          if x ! = y:
              combs . append ((x, y))
combs
```

Note. Note that the order of the instructions for and if is the same in these different code snippets.

The break instruction

The break statement causes an immediate exit from a loop while or loop for.

In the following example, the expression True is always ... true: we have an endless loop.

Instruction break is the only way out of the loop.

Example: Displaying the current time

```
import  time         # import module time
while   True :
     # strftime () is a function of time module
     print ( "current time" , time . strftime ( '% H:% M:% S' ))
     quit =  input ( 'Do you want to quit the program (o / n)?' )
      if quit ==  'o' :
          break
print ( "See you soon" )
```

Trick

If you know the number of loops to make, use a loop for. Otherwise, use a loop while (especially to make endless loops).

The functions

We have already seen a lot of functions: `print()`, `type()`, `len()`, `input()`, `range()`...

These are pre-defined functions (Native functions).

We also have the opportunity to create our own functions!

Interest of the functions

A function is a portion of code that can be called as needed (it's a kind of subroutine).

The use of functions avoids redundancies in the code: thus shorter and more readable programs are obtained.

For example, we need to repeatedly convert from degrees Celsius to degrees Fahrenheit: $$ T\_F = T\_C \times 1.8 + 32 $$

```
print ( 100  *  1.8  +  32.0 )

print ( 37.0  *  1.8  +  32.0 )

print ( 233.0  *  1.8  +  32.0 )
```

The same thing using a function:

```
def  fahrenheit (degree_celsius):

        " "  "

        Convert degree Celsius to degree Fahrenheit

        "  " "

        print (degree_celsius *  1.8  +  32.0 )

fahrenheit ( 100 )

fahrenheit ( 37 )

temperature =  220

fahrenheit (temperature)
```

The def instruction

Syntax

```
def  function-name (parameter1, parameter2, parameter3, ... ):

    """

    Documentation

    that can be written

    on several lines

    " ""        # 3 docstring surrounded by quotes (or quotes)


    "instruction block"        # attention to indentation


    return result              # the function returns the contents of
    the result variable
```

Example

```
def  myfirstfunction ():          # this function has no parameter

    """

    This function displays 'Hello'

    " ""

    print ( "Hello" )

    return                        # this function returns nothing
    ('None')

    # the return statement is here optional
mapremierefonction ()
help (mapremierefonction)
```

Scripts

Let's start by writing a script, that is, a file with a sequence of instructions to execute each time the script is called. The instructions can be, for example, copied and pasted from a **code cell** into your notebook (but be sure to follow the indentation rules!).

The extension for Python files is .py. Write or copy and paste the following lines into a file called test.py

```
string = 'Good evening'

for letter in string:    # letter is the iteration variable

    print (letter)
```

Now let's run the script interactively, inside the Ipython interpreter (notebook code cell). This is perhaps the most common use of scripts in computation and scientific simulation.

Note In the code (Ipython) cell , the syntax for running a script is %run script.py. For example:

```
% run test . py

chain
```

The syntax for loading the contunu of a script into a code cell is %load script.py. For example:

```
#% load test.py

string = 'Good evening'

for letter in string:    # letter is the iteration variable

    print (letter)
```

Basic Data structures

This chapter describes in more detail some things you have already seen and adds some new things.

The lists

The `` list '' data type has some more methods. These are all the methods of the list objects:

append (*x*)

> Add an element to the end of a list; is equivalent to .
> `a[len(a):] = [x]`

extend (*L*)

> Extend the list by concatenating all the elements of the indicated list; is equivalent to `a[len(a):] = L.`

insert (*i, x*)

> Insert an element in a given position. The first argument is the index of the element before it is inserted, so it `a.insert(0, x)` inserts at the beginning of the list and `a.insert(len(a), x)` equals `a.append(x).`

remove (*x*)

> Remove the first item from the list whose value it is `x`. It causes an error if there is no such element.

pop ([*i*])

> Remove the item from the given position in the list and return it. If an index is not specified, it `a.pop()` returns the last item in the list and also deletes it. The brackets surrounding the *i* in the method signature indicate that the parameter is optional, not that the brackets must be typed in that position.

index (*x*)

> Returns the index of the first item in the list whose value is x. It causes an error if there is no such element.

count (*x*)

> Returns the number of times that appears xin the list.

sort ()

> Sorts the elements of the list itself (the list is changed).

reverse ()

> Inverts the list itself (the list is changed).

An example that uses several methods in the list:

```
>>> a = [66.25, 333, 333, 1, 1234.5]
>>> print a.count (333), a.count (66.25), a.count ('x')
2 1 0
>>> a.insert (2, -1)
>>> a.append (333)
>>> a
[66.25, 333, -1, 333, 1, 1234.5, 333]
>>> a.index (333)
one
>>> a.remove (333)
>>> a
[66.25, -1, 333, 1, 1234.5, 333]
>>> a.reverse ()
>>> a
[333, 1234.5, 1, 333, -1, 66.25]
>>> a.sort ()
>>> a
[-1, 1, 66.6, 333, 333, 1234.5]
```

How to use lists as stacks

The methods of the lists make it much easier to use a list as a stack, where the last element added is the first item recovered. (`` last-in, first-out ", `` last to arrive, first to exit "). To stack an element, useappend

() . To recover the top element of the stack, use `pop` () without an explicit index. For example:

```
>>> pile = [3, 4, 5]
>>> pila.append (6)
>>> pila.append (7)
>>> stack
[3, 4, 5, 6, 7]
>>> pila.pop ()
7
>>> stack
[3, 4, 5, 6]
>>> pila.pop ()
6
>>> pila.pop ()
5
>>> stack
[3. 4]
```

How to use lists as queues

It is also very practical to use a list as a queue, where the first element that is added to the queue is the first one to leave (`` first-in, first-out ", `` first to arrive, last to exit ") . To add an element to the end of a queue, use `append` () . To retrieve the first element of the queue, use `pop` () with the 0index. For example:

```
>>> tail = ["Eric", "John", "Michael"]
>>> cola.append ("Terry") # arrives Terry
>>> cola.append ("Graham") # Graham arrives
>>> cola.pop (0)
'Eric'
>>> cola.pop (0)
'John'
>>> tail
['Michael', 'Terry', 'Graham']
```

Functional programming tools

There are three internal functions that are very useful when dealing with lists: `filter ()` , `map ()` and `reduce ()` .

" `filter ( function , sequence )` ", filter, returns a sequence (of the same type, if possible) that contains those elements of the input sequence for which it is true. For example, to calculate some cousins: *función (elemento)*

```
>>> def f (x): return x% 2! = 0 and x% 3! = 0
...
>>> filter (f, range (2, 25))
[5, 7, 11, 13, 17, 19, 23]
```

" `map ( function , sequence )` ", transform, call a for each of the elements of the sequence and return a list composed of the resulting values. For example, to calculate some cubes: *función (elemento)*

```
>>> def cube (x): return x * x * x
...
>>> map (cube, range (1, 11))
[1, 8, 27, 64, 125, 216, 343, 512, 729, 1000]
```

More than one sequence can be passed as a parameter. The function must have as many arguments as sequences are passed to it and the function is called with the corresponding value of each input sequence (or `None` if one sequence is shorter than another). For example:

```
>>> sequence = range (8)
>>> def sum (x, y): return x + y
...
>>> map (sum, sequence, sequence)
[0, 2, 4, 6, 8, 10, 12, 14]
```

" `reduce ( func , sequence )` ", reduce, return a simple value that is constructed by calling the binary function *func* with the first two elements of the sequence, then with the result and the next element and so on. For example, to calculate the sum of the numbers from 1 to 10:

```
>>> def sum (x, y): return x + y
...
```

57

```
>>> reduce (sum, range (1, 11))
55
```

If there is only one element in the sequence, its value is returned; if the sequence is empty, an exception is thrown.

A third argument can be passed to indicate the initial value. In this case, this initial value is returned for the empty sequence and the function is applied to the first element, then to the second, and so on. For example,

```
>>> def sum (sequence):
... def sum (x, y): return x + y
... return reduces (sum, sequence, 0)
...
>>> sum (range (1, 11))
55
>>> sum ([])
0
```

Do not use the `sum ()` function of this example: as adding numbers is a common task, an internal function is provided that does this exactly. New in version 2.3. `sum`

Self-defined lists

Self-defined lists provide a concise way to create lists without resorting to `map ()` , `filter ()` or `lambda` . The definition of the resulting list tends to be clearer than the lists built with the cited methods. Each LC consists of an expression followed by a `for` clause and zero or more `for` or `if` clauses . The resulting list is obtained by evaluating the expression in the context of the `for` and `if` clauses that follow it. If the expression must result in a tuple, it must be enclosed in parentheses.

```
>>> frutafresca = ['banana', 'mora', 'passion fruit']
>>> [arma.strip () for arma in frutafresca]
['plantain', 'mora', 'passion fruit']
>>> vec = [2, 4, 6]
>>> [3 * x for x in vec]
[6, 12, 18]
>>> [3 * x for x in vector if x> 3]
```

```
[12, 18]
>>> [3 * x for x in vec if x <2]
[]
>>> [[x, x ** 2] for x in vec]
[[2, 4], [4, 16], [6, 36]]
>>> [x, x ** 2 for x in vec] # error - a parenthesis is
needed in the tuples
  File "<stdin>", line 1, in?
    [x, x ** 2 for x in vec]
                 ^
SyntaxError: invalid syntax
>>> [(x, x ** 2) for x in vec]
[(2, 4), (4, 16), (6, 36)]
>>> vec1 = [2, 4, 6]
>>> vec2 = [4, 3, -9]
>>> [x * y for x in vec1 for and in vec2]
[8, 6, -18, 16, 12, -36, 24, 18, -54]
>>> [x + y for x in vec1 for and in vec2]
[6, 5, -7, 8, 7, -5, 10, 9, -3]
>>> [vec1 [i] * vec2 [i] for i in range (len (vec1))]
[8, 12, -54]
>>> [vec1 [i] * vec2 [i] for i in range (len (vec1))]
[8, 12, -54]
```

Self - defined lists are much more lexibles that `map` `()` and can be applied to functions with more than one argument and to nested functions:

```
>>> [str (round (355 / 113.0, i)) for i in range (1,6)]
['3.1', '3.14', '3.142', '3.1416', '3.14159']
```

The ruling of the

There is a way to remove an item from a given its index instead of its value list: the judgment of . It can also be used to remove cuts from a list (what we did earlier by assigning an empty list to the cut). For example:

```
>>> a = [-1, 1, 66.25, 333, 333, 1234.5]
>>> from to [0]
>>> a
```

```
[1, 66.25, 333, 333, 1234.5]
>>> from to [2: 4]
>>> a
[1, 66.25, 1234.5]
```

`the` can be used to delete entire variable:

```
>>> of the a
```

Referencing the name `a` from here causes an error (at least until another value is assigned to the name). We will see other uses of `the` later.

Tuples and sequences

We have seen that lists and chains have many properties in common, for example, indexing and cutting. They are two examples of *sequential* data types . Because Python is an evolving language, other types of sequence data can be added. There is another type of standard sequential data: the *tuple* .

A tuple consists of a certain number of values separated by commas, for example:

```
>>> t = 12345, 54321, 'hello!'
>>> t [0]
12345
>>> t
(12345, 54321, 'hello!')
>>> # Tuples can be nested:
... u = t, (1, 2, 3, 4, 5)
>>> u
((12345, 54321, 'hello!'), (1, 2, 3, 4, 5))
```

As you can see, in the output the tuples are enclosed in parentheses, so that the nested tuples are interpreted correctly. At the entrance the parentheses are optional, although they are often necessary (if the tuple is part of a more complex expression).

Tuples are very useful: For example, pairs of coordinates (x, y), records of employees in a database, etc. The tuples, like the chains, are immutable: It is not possible to assign a value to the individual elements of a tuple (however, the same effect can be simulated by cutting and concatenation). It is also possible to create tuples that contain mutable objects, for example, lists.

A special problem is the construction of tuples of 0 or 1 elements: The syntax has tricks to solve this. Empty tuples are constructed by a pair of empty parentheses and the tuples of a single element are constructed by the value of the element followed by a comma (it is not worth enclosing the value in parentheses). It's ugly, but it works. For example:

```
>>> empty = ()
>>> singleton = 'hello', # <- Observe the final comma
>>> len (empty)
0
>>> len (singleton)
one
>>> singleton
('Hello',)
```

The sentence t = 12345, 54321, '¡hola!' is an example of *tuple packaging* : the values 12345, 54321 and they '¡hola!' are packaged in a tuple. The reverse operation can also be performed:

```
>>> x, y, z = t
```

This is called, of course, *unpacking of sequences* . The unpacking of sequences requires that the number of variables be equal to the number of elements of the sequence. Note that multiple allocation is only a combined effect of tuple packaging and unpacking of sequences.

This is a little asymmetrical, since the packaging of several values always results in a tuple, although the unpacking works for any sequence.

Sets

Python also includes a data type for the *sets* . A set is a messy collection without duplicate elements. Basic uses include checking membership and removing duplicate items. The joint objects also have mathematical operations such as union, intersection, difference and symmetric difference.

Here is a brief demonstration:

```
>>> basket = ['apple', 'orange', 'apple', 'pear', 'orange',
'banana']
>>> fruits = set (basket) # create a set without
duplicates
>>> fruits
set (['orange', 'pear', 'apple', 'banana'])
>>> 'orange' in fruits # quick check of membership
True
>>> 'nettles' in fruits
False

>>> # Demonstration of set operations on two-word letters

>>> a = set ('abracadabra')
>>> b = set ('alacazam')
>>> a # different letters from to
set (['a', 'r', 'b', 'c', 'd'])
>>> a - b # a letters that are not in b
set (['r', 'd', 'b'])
>>> a | b # letters that are in a or b
set (['a', 'c', 'r', 'd', 'b', 'm', 'z', 'l'])
>>> a & b # letters that are in ay also in b
set (['a', 'c'])
>>> a ^ b # letters that are in a and b but not in both
set (['r', 'd', 'b', 'm', 'z', 'l'])
```

Dictionaries

Another type of Python internal data that is useful is the <u>dictionary</u>. Dictionaries sometimes appear in other languages such as `` associative memories " or `` associative matrices ". Unlike sequences, which are indexed by a range of numbers, dictionaries are indexed by *keys* , which can be of any immutable type. You can always use strings and numbers as keys. Tuples can be used as keys if they contain only strings, numbers or tuples. If a tuple contains any mutable object directly or indirectly, it can not be used as a key. Lists can not be used as keys, since lists can be modified, for example, by the `append ()` method and its `extend ()` method, in addition to cutting assignments and increased assignments.

It is best to think of a dictionary as a messy set of *key* pairs *: value* , with the requirement that the keys be unique (within the same dictionary). A pair of braces creates an empty dictionary `{}`. If a list of *key : value* pairs is placed between the keys, initial *key : value* pairs are added to the dictionary. This is how the dictionaries are presented in the output (there are examples shortly).

The main operations on a dictionary are to store a value with a given key and to extract the value from the key. You can also remove a *key : value* pair with `del`. If you enter a key that already exists, the previous value is forgotten. Trying to extract a value using a non-existent key causes an error.

The `keys ()` method of a dictionary-type object returns all the keys used in the dictionary, in arbitrary order (if you want to sort them, apply the `sort ()` method to the list of keys). To check if a key exists in the dictionary, use the `has_key ()` method of the dictionary.

Here is a small example that uses a dictionary:

```
>>> tel = {'jack': 4098, 'sape': 4139}
>>> tel ['guido'] = 4127
>>> tel
{'sape': 4139, 'guido': 4127, 'jack': 4098}
>>> tel ['jack']
4098
>>> from the tel ['sape']
>>> tel ['irv'] = 4127
>>> tel
{'guido': 4127, 'irv': 4127, 'jack': 4098}
>>> tel.keys ()
['guido', 'irv', 'jack']
>>> tel.has_key ('guido')
True
```

The `dict` () constructor builds dictionaries directly from lists of key-value pairs saved as tuples. When couples meet a pattern, the list of key-value pairs can be specified in a compact manner.

```
>>> dict ([('sape', 4139), ('guido', 4127), ('jack', 4098)])
{'sape': 4139, 'jack': 4098, 'guido': 4127}
>>> dict ([(x, x ** 2) for x in (2, 4, 6)]) # use of self-defined list
{2: 4, 4: 16, 6: 36}
```

Later in this guide, we will know the generating expressions, which are even more suitable for the task of providing key-value pairs to the `dict` () constructor .

Techniques for looping

When traversing dictionaries, it is possible to recover the key and its corresponding value at the same time, using the `iteritems` () method .

```
>>> knights = {'gallahad': 'the chaste', 'robin': 'the courageous'}
>>> for k, v in caballeros.iteritems ():
... print k, v
...
gallahad the chaste
robin the brave
```

By traversing a sequence, the position index and its corresponding value can be retrieved at the same time by using the `enumerate` () function .

```
>>> for i, v in enumerate (['pim', 'pam', 'pum']):
... print i, v
...
0 pim
1 pam
2 pum
```

To run two or more sequences in parallel, you can match the values with the `zip ()` function .

```
>>> questions = ['name', 'mission', 'favorite color']
>>> answers = ['lanzarote', 'the holy grail', 'blue']
>>> for p, r in zip (questions, answers):
... print 'What is your% s? % s. ' % (p, r)
...
What is your name? lanzarote.
What is your mission? The Holy Grail.
What is your favorite color? blue.
        <
```

To traverse a sequence in reverse order, you must first specify the sequence in the original order and call the function `reversed ()` .

```
>>> for i in reversed (xrange (1,10,2)):
... print i
...
9
7
5
3
one
```

To traverse a sequence in order, use the `sorted ()` function , which returns a new sorted list, leaving the original sequence intact.

```
>>> basket = ['apple', 'orange', 'apple', 'orange', 'pear',
'banana']
>>> for f in sorted (set (basket)):
... print f
...
banana
Apple
orange
pear
```

More about the conditions

The conditions used in buildings `while` and `if` described above may contain any operator, not only comparisons.

The comparison operators `in`(inside) and `not in`(not inside) check whether a value is included (or not) in a sequence. The operators `is`(es) and `is not`(is not) check if two objects are actually the same. This only matters in mutable objects, such as lists. All comparison operators have the same priority, which is less than that of the numeric operators.

You can link the comparisons: For example, `a < b == c` check if it `a` is less than `b`and also if it `b` is equal to `c`.

Comparisons can be combined using the logical operators `and`(y) and `or`(o) and the output of a comparison (or any other logical expression) can be denied by `not`(no). All these have lower priority than comparison operators. Among them, it `not` has the highest priority and `or` the lowest, so it `A and not B or C` equals `(A and (not B)) or C`. As always, parentheses can be used to express a particular order of operation.

The logical operators `and` and `or` are called *short - circuit* operators : Their arguments are evaluated from left to right and the evaluation is interrupted as soon as the output value is determined. For example, if it `A` has a value of true but `B` is false, it `A and B and C` does not evaluate the value of expression C. In general, the value returned by a shortcut operator, when used as a value in general and not as a logical value, is the last evaluated argument.

It is possible to assign the result of a comparison or other logical expression to a variable. For example:

```
>>> string1, string2, string3 = '', 'Trondheim', 'Hammer
Dance'
>>> non_null = string1 or string2 or string3
>>> non_null
'Trondheim'
```

Note that in Python, unlike in C, there can be no assignment within an expression. Programmers in C may complain about this, but avoid a

66

common cause problems found in programs in C: type =in an expression that was meant ==.

Comparison between sequences and other types

The sequence objects can be compared with other objects of the same sequence type. The comparison uses *lexicographical* ordering: First the first two elements are compared, if these differ, the comparison value is already determined, if not, the next two elements of each sequence are compared, and so on, until one of the two sequences is exhausted. If any of the elements being compared is itself a sequence, a nested lexicographic comparison is carried out. If all the elements are equal, the sequences are considered equal. If one of the sequences is equal to the other truncated from a certain element, the shorter sequence of the two is the smaller one. The lexicographical ordering for the strings uses the order of the ASCII codes of their characters. Here are examples of comparisons between sequences of the same type:

```
(1, 2, 3) < (1, 2, 4)
[1, 2, 3] < [1, 2, 4]
'ABC' < 'C' < 'Pascal' < 'Python'
(1, 2, 3, 4) < (1, 2, 4)
(1, 2) < (1, 2, -1)
(1, 2, 3) == (1.0, 2.0, 3.0)
(1, 2, ('aa', 'ab')) < (1, 2, ('abc', 'a'), 4)
```

Note that it is legal to compare objects of different types. The result is deterministic but arbitrary: the types are ordered by name. In this way, a list is always less than a chain, a chain is always less than a tuple, etc. [5.1] The numerical values of different types are compared by their numerical value, so 0 equals 0.0, etc.

Functions

We've already seen a lot of functions: `print()`, `type()`, `len()`, `input()`, `range()`...
These are built-in functions .
We also have the opportunity to create our own functions!

Interest of the functions

A function is a portion of code that can be called as needed (it's a kind of subroutine).

The use of functions avoids redundancies in the code: thus shorter and more readable programs are obtained.

For example, we need to repeatedly convert from degrees Celsius to degrees Fahrenheit:

```
>>> print (100.0 * 9.0 / 5.0 + 32.0)
212.0
>>> print (37.0 * 9.0 / 5.0 + 32.0)
98.6
>>> print (233.0 * 9.0 / 5.0 + 32.0)
451.4
```

The same thing using a function:

```
>>> def fahrenheit (degre_celsius):
        "" "Convert degree Celsius to degree Fahrenheit" ""
        print (degree_celsius * 9.0 / 5.0 + 32.0)
>>> fahrenheit (100)
212.0
>>> fahrenheit (37)
98.6
```

```
>>> temperature = 233
>>> fahrenheit (temperature)
451.4
```

Nothing forces you to define functions in your scripts, but it is so convenient that it would be unproductive to do without!

The instruction def

Syntax

```
def        function-name      (parameter1,
parameter2, parameter3, ...):
"" "Documentation
we can write
on multiple lines "" "      #      docstring
surrounded by 3 quotation marks (or
apostrophes)


    instruction block        # attention
to indentation


    return result            #         the
function returns the contents of the
result variable
```

Example 1

```
# script Function1.py


def myfirstfunction ():    #         this
function has no parameter
```

```
    "" "This function displays 'Hello'"
""

    print ("Hello")

    return                    #           this
function returns nothing ('None')

                    #      the      return
statement is here optional
```

Once the function has been defined, we can call it:

```
>>> myfirstfunction()  # do not forget
parentheses ()
Hello
```

Access to the documentation is done with the pre-defined function help():

```
>>> help (myfirstname)        # displaying
the documentation

Help on function myfirstfunction in
module __main__:


myfirstfunction()
    This function displays 'Hello'
```

Example 2

The following function simulates the behavior of a 6-sided die. For this, we use the function randint()of the module **random**.

```
# script Function2.py


def draw_de ():
```

```python
        "" "Returns a random integer between
1 and 6" ""

    import random

    value = random.randint (1, 6)

    return value
>>> print (print_of ())
 3

>>> print (print_of ())
 6

>>> result = print_of ()
 >>> print (result)
 1
```

Example 3

```python
# script Function3.py


#file  info definition ():
    "" "Information" ""

    print ("q key to exit")
    print ("Enter key to continue")


def  draw_de ():
    "" "Returns a random integer between
1 and 6" ""
```

```
    import random
    value = random.randint (1, 6)
    return value

# beginning of the program
info ()
while  True :
    choice = input ()
     if choice == 'q' :
          break
    print ( "Draw:" , draw_of ())
>>>
q key to quit
Enter key to continue


Edition: 5


Edition: 6
q
>>>
```

Example 4

A function with two parameters:

```
# script Function4.py
```

72

```
# Definition of function
def   print_de2 (value_min, value_max):
    "" "Returns a random integer between
value_min and value_max" ""

    import random

    return   random.randint   (value_min,
value_max)


# start of the program
for i in   range (5):

    print (print_de2 (1, 10))    # call
of the function with arguments 1 and 10
>>>
6

7

1

10

2

>>>
```

Example 5

A function that returns a list:

```
# script Function5.py


# Definition function
```

```python
def print_multiple_de (nombretirage):
    "" "Returns a list of random integers between 1 and 6" ""

    import random

    result = [random.randint (1, 6) for i in range (counting)]   #   list comprehension (see appendix)

    return result


# start of the

print program (multiple_drawing_of (10))
>>>
[4, 1, 3, 3, 2, 1, 6, 6, 2, 5]
>>> help (multiple_drawing)
 Help on function draw_multiple_de in module __main__:


tirage_multiple_de (nombretirage)
    Returns a list of random integers between 1 and 6
```

Example 6

A function that displays the parity of an integer. There may be several instructions **return** in a function. The instruction **return** causes the immediate return of the function.

```python
# script Function6.py
```

74

```
# Definition of function
def  parity (number):
    ""  "Displays  the  parity  of  an
integer" ""
    if count% 2 == 1:    # The% operator
gives the remainder of a division
        print (number, is odd ' )
        return
    if number% 2 == 0:
        print (number, ' is even ' )
        return
>>> parity (13)
 13 is odd
>>> parity (24)
 24 is even
```

Scope of variables: global and local variables

The *scope of a variable* is the place in the program where you can access the variable.

Let's look at the following script:

```
a = 10            #  global  variable  in
the program

def  myfunction ():
    a = 20  # local variable to
    print (a)
```

```
    return function
```

```
>>> print (a)          # we are in the
global space of the program
```

```
10
```

```
>>> myfunction ()      # we are in the
local space of function
```

```
20
```

```
>>> print (a)          # back in space
global
```

```
10
```

We have two different variables that have the same name a

A variable a of value 20 is created in the function: it is a *variable local* to the function.
It is destroyed as soon as one leaves the function.

global

The statement **global** makes a global variable:

```
a = 10              # global variable
```

```
def mafunction ():
    global a        # the variable is now
global
    a = 20
    print (a)
    return
```

```
>>> print (a)
 10
```

```
>>> mafunction ()
 20
>>>  print (a)
 20
```

Note: it is better to avoid the use of the instruction global because it is a source of errors (one can thus modify the contents of a global variable by believing to act on a local variable).
Wisdom therefore recommends following the following rule:

- never assign a variable of the same name in a local code block as a global variable

Appendix: understanding of lists

The *understanding of lists* is a syntactic structure available in a number of programming languages, including Python. It's a way to efficiently create lists.

Let's go back to the example seen in the script Fonction5.py:

```
result  = [ random . randint ( 1 , 6 )
for  i  in  range ( 10 )]
>>>  print (result)
 [3, 1, 5, 6, 4, 2, 1, 1, 3, 1]
```

Another example: list of squares

```
squares  = [ i * i  for  i  in  range
( 11 )]
>>>  print (squares)
 [0, 1, 4, 9, 16, 25, 36, 49, 64, 81, 100]
```

Understanding lists therefore avoids writing the following "classic" code:

```
squares                                    = []
for      i     in     range  (  11  ):
    squares . append ( i * i )
```

Classes and Modules

The **class** is a basic concept of **object-oriented programming** .
In Python, you can write a script without defining classes (that's what we've done so far).
However, you must manipulate **objects (or class instances)** : an integer variable is an instance of the class `int`, a string is an instance of the class `str`...
The module `Tkinter`(which we will discuss in Chapter 7) is used to create graphical interfaces: this module provides a class   library.
It is therefore important to study classes in particular to understand how to use them (for a beginner, it's confusing!).

This section is quite difficult: I advise you to read again what we saw in Variables, data and operators.

Definition of a class

Here is an example of a script that uses a user-defined class.

We will start by creating the source file `BankAccount.py` (we will talk about the module later `BankAccount`):

Open IDLE:
Start → Programs → Python → IDLE (Python GUI)

File → New Window
Copy and paste the source code below:

```python
# - * - coding: utf-8 - * -
# BankAccount.py

# class definition Account

class  Account :
    "" "An example class:
    management of a bank account ""

    #defining the special method __init__
    def  __init__ (self, balanceInitial):
        "" "Initializing the account with
the balanceInitial value." ""
        # assigning the instance attribute
balance
        self.solde              =              float
(balanceInitial)

    #definition of the NewSale () method
    def  NewSolde (self, sum):
        "" "New account balance with sum
value." ""
        self.solde = float (sum)

    #definition of the method Balance ()
```

```python
def  Balance (self):
    "" "Returns the balance." ""
    return self.solde


# Credit method definition ()
def  Credit (self, sum):
    "" "Credits the sum value account.
Returns the balance." ""
    self.solde + = sum
    return self.solde


# Debit () method definition
def  Debit (self, sum):
    "" "Debit the count of the sum
value, return the balance." ""
    self.solde - = sum
    return self.solde


#defining the special method __add__
(operator overload +)
def  __add__ (self, sum):
    "" "x .__ add __ (sum) <=> x + sum
    Credits the sum value account.
    'New balance: sum' "" "poster
    self.solde + = sum
```

```python
        print ( "New balance: {: +. 2f}
€" .format (self.solde))
        return self


    #definition of the special method
__sub__ (operator overload -)
    def __sub__ (self, sum):
        "" "x .__ sub_ (sum) <=> x-sum
        Debits the account of the sum value.
        'New balance: sum' "" "poster
        self.solde - = sum
        print ( "New balance: {: +. 2f}
€" .format (self.solde))
        return self


if __name__ == '__main__' :
    # This statement block is executed if
the module is started as a standalone
program
    # Instantiation of the cb1 object of
the class Account
    cb1 = Account (1000)
    # Formatting data to display two
decimal places and the sign
    print ( "{.} + 2f" .format (cb1.Solde
()))
```

```
    print    (    "{.}   +    2f"    .format
(cb1.Credit (200)))
    print    (    "{:   +   .2f  }"    .format
(cb1.Debit (50.23)))
    print ( "{: +. 2f}" .format (cb1.Side
()))
    cb1.NouveauSolde (5100)
    print ( "{: +. 2f}" .format (cb1.Sound
()))
    cb1 + 253.2
    cb1-1000 + 100
    cb1-cb1.Solde ()
```

File → Save As
Directory: C: \ PythonXX
File Name: BankAccount.py

Then run the module:
Run → Run Module (or key F5):

```
>>>
+1000.00
+1200.00
+1149.77
+1149.77
+5100.00
New balance: +5353.20 €
New balance: +4353.20 €
New balance: +4453.20 €
```

```
New balance: +0.00 €
```
>>>

To define the new class Account, we use the instruction class.
A class has functions that we call **methods** and data that we call **attributes** .

A method is defined in the same way as a function (we start with the instruction def).
A method has at least one parameter called self.
The parameter self designates all the instances that will be created by this class.

7 methods are thus defined.

Only one instance attribute is used in this class: solde(not to be confused with the method Solde()).

The special method *__init__()*

The special method __init__()is executed automatically when you instantiate (create) a new object of the class. This method is similar to a constructor.

Other special methods

Two other special methods are used: __add__()and __sub__().

The writing cb1+253.2is equivalent to the cb1.__add__(253.2)
operator + represents here an addition on the balance.
The writing cb1–1000is equivalent to cb1.__sub__(1000)
The operator - here represents a subtraction on the balance.

>>> cb1.NewSolde (500)

 >>> print (cb1.Solde ())

```
500.0
>>> cb1 .__ add __ (1000)
 New balance: +1500.00 €
>>> cb1 + 2000      # this writing is very
practical!
 New balance: +3500.00 €
>>>
```

The instruction *if __name__ == '__main__':*

Here, the module is executed as a main program: the following instructions are executed. In case this module is imported into another program, this part of the code has no effect.

Documentation

The function help() is very useful.
We understand here the interest of well documenting its programs with """docstrings""":

```
>>>  help (cb1)
 Help on instance of Account in module
__main__:


class Account
 | An example of class:
 | management of a bank account
 |
 | Methods defined here:
 |
```

| Credit (self, sum)

| Credits the sum value account. Returns
the balance.

|

| Debit (self, sum)

| Debits the account of the sum value.
Returns the balance.

|

| NewSolde (self, sum)

| New account balance with the sum value.

|

| Balance (self)

| Returns the balance.

|

| __add __ (self, sum)

| x .__ add __ (sum) <=> x + sum

| Credits the sum value account.

| 'New balance: sum' poster

|

| __init __ (self, initial balance)

| Initialization of the account with
balanceInitial.

|

| __sub __ (self, sum)

| x .__ sub_ (sum) <=> x-sum

```
| Debits the account of the sum value.
| 'New balance: sum' poster
>>>
```

The function dir()returns the list of methods and attributes:

```
>>>   dir (cb1)
 ['Credit',       'Debit',       'NewSolde',
'Balance', '__add__',
'__doc__',     '__init__',     '__module__',
'__sub__', 'balance']
```

Remarks

We can instantiate several objects of the same class:

```
>>> cb2 = Account (10000)
 >>>   print (cb2.Credit (500))
 10500.0
>>> cb3 = Account (6000)       #    and    one
more!
>>> cb3-500
 New balance: +5500.00 €
>>>
```

Although this is not advisable, you can directly access the instance attributes:

```
>>>   print (cb2.solde)
 10500.0
>>> cb2.solde = 5000.0       # assignment
of instance attribute balance
```

```
>>>    print (cb2.solde)
 5000.0
>>>    print (cb2.Solde ())
 5000.0
>>>
```

Note that mechanisms are provided to customize the access mode to attributes: function **property()** or decorator **@property**

Importing a user-defined module

The import of our personal module **CompteBancaire** is done in the same way as for the basic modules (**math, random, time**...).

Restart the Python Shell:
Shell → Restart Shell

```
>>>    import BankAccount
 >>>  cb = BankAccount.Count (1500)
 >>>   print (cb.Debit (200))
 1300.0
>>>   print (cb.solde)
 1300.0
>>> cb + 2000
 New balance: +3300.00 €
>>>
```

The module **BankAccount** is imported by the main program (here the interactive interpreter). The part of the code that follows the instruction **if** `__name__ == '__main__':` is ignored (so there is no display after the statement `import BankAccount`).

Class Modules, Function Modules

IDLE has the tool **Path Browser** to know the structure of a module.

File → Path Browser

A module can contain classes (`BankAccount`), functions (<u>`animation`</u>) or functions and classes.

Another example

The standard module `math` is a function module. To convince yourself of this:

```
>>>   import math
>>>   help (math)
Help on built-in math module:


NAME
    math


FILE
    (Built-in)


DESCRIPTION
    This module is always available. It
provides   access   to   the   mathematical
functions defined by the standard C.
```

FUNCTIONS

acos (...)

acos (x)

Return the arc cosine (measured
in radians) of x.

acosh (...)

acosh (x)

Return the hyperbolic arc cosine
(measured in radians) of x.

...

...

trunc (...)

trunc (x: Real) -> Integral

Truncates x to the nearest
Integral to 0. Uses the __trunc__ magic
method.

DATA

e = 2.718281828459045

```
    pi = 3.141592653589793
```

The module math also has two data (pi and e):

```
>>>  print (math.e)            # data e of
the math module (Euler number)
```

2.71828182846

```
>>>  print (math.pi)           # pi data of
the math module (pi number)
```

3.14159265359

```
>>>  print (math.sin (math.pi / 4.0))   #
function sin () of the math module (sine)
```

0.707106781187

```
>>>  print (math.sqrt (2.0))       #
function sqrt () of the math module
(square root)
```

1.41421356237

```
>>>  print ( math.exp (-3.0))      #
function exp () of the math module
(exponential)
```

0.0497870683679

```
>>>  print (math.log (math.e))   # log ()
function of the math module (natural
logarithm)
```

1.0

Iterators

To understand the philosophy of the *Iterators* , look for the *simplicity* of the operations, avoiding the duplication of effort, which is a waste and seeks to replace several of the approaches with a standard feature, normally, derives in making things more readable more interoperable.

An iterator is an object attached to the iterator protocol , basically this means that it has a function *next ()* , that is, when it is called, it returns the next element in the sequence, when there is nothing left to be returned, it throws the exception *StopIteration* and it causes stopping the iteration. But if you call it explicitly you can see that, once the iterator is *exhausted* , when you call it again you will see that the exception mentioned above is thrown.

Next, the use of iterators using the special method __iter__() included in the *integrated object file* :

```
>>> file = open ( '/ etc / hostname' )

>>> file

<open file '/ etc / hostname', mode 'r' at
0x7fa44ba379c0>

>>> file . __iter__ ()

<open file '/ etc / hostname', mode 'r' at
0x7fa44ba379c0>

>>> iter ( file )

<open file '/ etc / hostname', mode 'r' at
0x7fa44ba379c0>

>>> file is file . __iter__ ()
```

```
True

>>> line = file . __iter__ ()

>>> line . next ()

'laptop \ n'

>>> line . next ()

Traceback (most recent call last):

    File "<stdin>" , line 1 , in <module>

StopIteration
```

In the example, the special __iter__ () method does the same thing as the built-in *iter (file) function.*

Iterators and sequences

Iterators are used with the standard sequence types. Here are some examples:

Iterate over the immutable string character string

Here is an example of the use of iterators with the *immutable string of* ASCII *character string* type:

```
>>> phrase = 'Hello World'

>>> letter = iter ( phrase )

>>> letter . next ()

'H'

>>> letter . next ()
```

```
'or'
>>> letter . next ()
'l'
>>> letter . next ()
'to'
>>> letter . next ()
' '
>>> letter . next ()
'M'
>>> letter . next ()
'or'
>>> letter . next ()
'n'
>>> letter . next ()
'd'
>>> letter . next ()
'or'
>>> letter . next ()
Traceback (most recent call last):
  File "<stdin>" , line 1 , in <module>
```

In the previous example, when iterating in the `frase` sequence, when reaching the end through the `letra` iterator, the *StopIteration* exception is *called* and the iteration is stopped.

Iterate over the unchanging sequence Unicode string

Here is an example of the use of iterators with the *unchanging* sequence of type `Unicode` *character string* :

```
>>> phrase = u'Jekechitü '
>>> letter = iter ( phrase )
>>> letter . next ()
u'J '
>>> letter . next ()
EU'
>>> letter . next ()
u'k '
>>> letter . next ()
EU'
>>> letter . next ()
u'c '
>>> letter . next ()
u'h '
```

```
>>> letter . next ()

u'i '

>>> letter . next ()

u't '

>>> letter . next ()

u '\ xfc'

>>> letter . next ()

Traceback (most recent call last):

   File "<stdin>" , line 1 , in <module>

StopIteration
```

In the previous example, when iterating in the frase sequence, when reaching the end through the letra iterator, the *StopIteration* exception is *called* and the iteration is stopped.

Iterate over the immutable tuple sequence

Here is an example of the use of iterators with the *immutable tuple-* type sequence:

```
>>> values = ( "Python" , True , "Zope" , 5 )

>>> values

('Python', True, "Zope", 5)

>>> values . __iter__ ()

<tupleiterator object at 0x7fa44b9fa450>
```

```
>>> value = values .   __iter__ ()

>>> value . next ()

'Python'

>>> value . next ()

True

>>> value . next ()

'Zope'

>>> value . next ()

5

>>> value . next ()

Traceback (most recent call last):

  File "<stdin>" , line 1 , in <module>

StopIteration
```

In the previous example, when iterating in the sequence valores , when reaching the end through the valor iterator, the *StopIteration* exception is *called* and the iteration is stopped.

Iterate over the immutable xrange function

Here is an example of the use of iterators with the *immutable* sequence with the built-in function *xrange ()* :

```
>>> list = iter ( xrange ( 5 ))

>>> list
```

```
<rangeiterator object at 0x7fa44b9fb7b0>
>>> list .  next ()
0
>>> list .  next ()
one
>>> list .  next ()
two
>>> list .  next ()
3
>>> list .  next ()
4
>>> list .  next ()
Traceback (most recent call last):
   File "<stdin>" , line 1 , in <module>
StopIteration
```

In the previous example, when iterating in the `lista` sequence, when the end is reached, the *StopIteration* exception is *called* and the iteration is stopped.

Iterate over the mutable sequence list

Here is an example of the use of iterators with the *mutable* sequence of type *list* :

```
>>> versions_plone = [ 2.1 , 2.5 , 3.6 , 4 , 5 , 6 ]
>>> iter ( versions_plone )
<listiterator object at 0x7fa44b9fa450>
>>> version = iter ( versions_plone )
>>> version
<listiterator object at 0x7fa44b9fa550>
>>> version . next ()
2.1
>>> version . next ()
2.5
>>> version . next ()
3.6
>>> version . next ()
4
>>> version . next ()
5
>>> version . next ()
6
>>> version . next ()
Traceback (most recent call last):
```

```
  File "<stdin>" , line 1 , in <module>
```

StopIteration

In the previous example, when you iterate in the sequence versiones_plone ,
when you reach the end using the version iterator, the *StopIteration* exception
is *called* and the iteration is stopped.

You can return an iterator object in reverse order over a *mutable* sequence of
type *list* using its built-in function __reversed__ () .

```
>>> versions_plone = [ 2.1 , 2.5 , 3.6 , 4 , 5 , 6 ]

>>> versions_plone . __reversed__ ()

<listreverseiterator object at 0xb712ebec>

>>> version = versions_plone . __reversed__ ()

>>> version . next ()

6

>>> version . next ()

5

>>> version . next ()

4

>>> version . next ()

3.6

>>> version . next ()

2.5
```

```
>>> version . next ()

2.1

>>> version . next ()

Traceback (most recent call last):

  File "<stdin>" , line 1 , in <module>

StopIteration
```

In the previous example, when you iterate in the sequence versiones_plone , when you reach the end using the version iterator, the *StopIteration* exception is *called* and the iteration is stopped.

You can also access the use of the special __iter__ () method included in the *mutable* sequence of the integrated *list* type:

```
>>> versions_plone = [ 2.1 , 2.5 , 3.6 , 4 , 5 , 6 ]

>>> versions_plone . __iter__ ()

<listiterator object at 0x7fa44b9fa510>
```

Iterate over the mutable range function

Here is an example of the use of iterators with the *mutable* sequence of the built-in function *range ()* :

```
>>> list = iter ( range ( 5 ))

>>> list

<listiterator object at 0x7fa44b9fa490>

>>> list . next ()
```

```
0

>>> list . next ()

one

>>> list . next ()

two

>>> list . next ()

3

>>> list . next ()

4

>>> list . next ()

Traceback (most recent call last):

    File "<stdin>" , line 1 , in <module>

StopIteration
```

In the previous example, when iterating in the lista sequence, when the end is reached, the *StopIteration* exception is *called* and the iteration is stopped.

Iterators and sets

Iterators are used with the standard set types. Here are some examples:

Iterate over the mutable set

Here is an example of the use of iterators with the *mutable* set of type *sets* :

```
>>> versions_plone = set ([ 2.1 , 2.5 , 3.6 , 4 , 5 ,
6 , 4 ])

>>> version = iter ( versions_plone )

>>> version

<setiterator object at 0x7fac9c7c7a50>

>>> version . next ()

2.5

>>> version . next ()

4

>>> version . next ()

5

>>> version . next ()

6

>>> version . next ()

2.1

>>> version . next ()

3.6

>>> version . next ()

Traceback (most recent call last):

  File "<stdin>" , line 1 , in <module>

StopIteration
```

In the previous example, when you iterate in the sequence `versiones_plone`, when you reach the end using the `version` iterator, the *StopIteration* exception is *called* and the iteration is stopped.

Iterate over the immutable set

Here is an example of the use of iterators with the *immutable* set of type *sets* :

```
>>> versions_plone = frozenset ([ 6 , 2.1 , 2.5 , 3.6 ,
4 , 5 , 4 , 2.5 ])

>>> version = iter ( versions_plone )

>>> version

<setiterator object at 0x7fac9c7c7cd0>

>>> version . next ()

2.5

>>> version . next ()

4

>>> version . next ()

5

>>> version . next ()

6

>>> version . next ()

2.1

>>> version . next ()
```

3.6

```
>>> version . next ()

Traceback (most recent call last):

  File "<stdin>" , line 1 , in <module>

StopIteration
```

In the previous example, when you iterate in the sequence `versiones_plone` , when you reach the end using the `version` iterator, the *StopIteration* exception is *called* and the iteration is stopped.

Iterators and mappings

Iterators are used with the standard sequence types. Here are some examples:

Iterate over dictionary keys

Next, an example of the use of the iterators with the *mapping* sequence, *dictionary* type, by default shows the key of the sequence:

```
  >>> versions_plone = dict ( python = 2.7 , zope = 2.13 ,
plone = 5.1 )

>>> package = iter ( versions_plone )

>>> package

<dictionary-keyiterator object at 0x7fa44b9e99f0>

>>> package . next ()

'zope'

>>> package . next ()
```

```
'python'

>>> package . next ()

'plone'

>>> package . next ()

Traceback (most recent call last):

   File "<stdin>" , line 1 , in <module>

StopIteration
```

In the previous example, when you iterate in the sequence versiones_plone ,
when you reach the end using the paquete iterator, the *StopIteration* exception
is *called* and the iteration is stopped.

Iterate over dictionary values

Next, an example of the use of iterators with the *mapping* sequence, *dictionary*
type to show the value of a key using the integrated method *itervalues ()* :

```
>>> versions_plone = dict ( python = 2.7 , zope = 2.13 ,
plone = 5.1 )

>>> version = iter ( versions_plone . itervalues ())

>>> version

<dictionary-valueiterator object at 0x7fa44b9e9c00>

>>> version . next ()

2.13

>>> version . next ()
```

```
2.7

>>> version . next ()

5.1

>>> version . next ()

Traceback (most recent call last):

    File "<stdin>" , line 1 , in <module>

StopIteration
```

In the previous example, when you iterate in the sequence versiones_plone , when you reach the end using the version iterator, the *StopIteration* exception is *called* and the iteration is stopped.

Iterate over the dictionary elements

Next, an example of the use of iterators with the *mapping* sequence, *dictionary* type to show the key / value pair using the built-in method *iteritems ()* :

```
>>> versions_plone = dict ( python = 2.7 , zope = 2.13 ,
plone = 5.1 )

>>> package = iter ( versions_plone . iteritems ())

>>> package

<dictionary-itemiterator object at 0x7fa44b9e9b50>

>>> package . next ()

('zope', 2.13)

>>> package . next ()
```

```
('python', 2.7)

>>> package . next ()

('plone', 5.1)

>>> package . next ()

Traceback (most recent call last):

   File "<stdin>" , line 1 , in <module>

StopIteration
```

In the previous example, when you iterate in the sequence versiones_plone ,
when you reach the end using the paquete iterator, the *StopIteration* exception
is *called* and the iteration is stopped.

Advanced Concepts - Suitable for Intermediate Level

Generators: What They Are And What Problems They Solve

The other day a friend saw me writing a function in Python that I
used yield instead of return and asked:

"How useful is that?" Never understood.

Actually I was writing a generator and not a function. The syntax is
basically the same, the only difference is what my friend noticed: o
yield instead of return. And so? What is it for?

A function returns a value and is ready, let's say that the beautiful
existence of this function in the world ends there. A generator does not,
it delivers you a value and keeps waiting for you to ask the next one.

For example, I can have a function that returns a list of numbers [1, 2, 3] and then I see what I do with them. A generator gives me the 1, and expects me to ask *and then generator, what next?*, there he gives me the 2 and so on.

But better than that, I think, is to go for a practical example: imagine a function, which returns all integers between 0 and max_number (ok, of course you can use the range direct, but ... just imagine):

```
def numbers_up_to(max_number):
    output = []

    for number in range(max_number + 1):
        output.append(number)

    return output
```

Writing this function creates a list [0, 1, 2, 3, 4, …] until you reach the max_number. It already creates this list, allocates it in memory, saving the entire list and its contents. It takes up space, uses hardware resources for it. And it does not have any problem if it max_number is small ...

... but try to use that function there with a mole, that is, with numbers_up_to(623 * 10 ** 21). No, do not try. Your computer will freak out. Seriously.

For this we have a more efficient alternative: generators! Let's turn this *function* into a *generator*. It's simple: we do not create any list and use it yield instead of return:

```
def numbers_up_to(max_number):
    for number in range(max_number + 1):
        yield number
```

Now try to use this function with the giant number: numbers_up_to_as(623 * 10 ** 21). Go with faith. This time you can try. Your computer will not work like this.

It will only calculate the first element of the sequence when you need it. And it will deliver 1 and stop you. It does not process anything, it does not allocate anything in memory. Until you ask for the next number. Then he forgets the first and hands you the second. And so it goes. You go ordering and he goes handing one at a time, the third, then the fourth, then the fifth, and so on. One at a time.

Instead of creating the whole list, it creates a generator (of lists, for example, but an iterable one) and calculates one by one the elements, according to the need to access them ... and in fact it will only calculate some thing every `next()`- that is the function called internally if you pass a generator to one `for`, for example.

But `next()` it can also be used manually - which is great for exploring:

```
my_first_generator = numbers_up_to(42)
next(my_first_generator)
next(my_first_generator)
next(my_first_generator)
next(my_first_generator)
next(my_first_generator)
```

In my examples, even `range` what is native to Python 3 is already a generator itself.

Generators are very useful and very kind to memory. But since they are not all flowers, of course, they have some limitations: for example, you can not use two `for` on the same generator directly - generators only advance in sequence, never return to the beginning of it. So when the first one `for` depletes the generator, the second `for` will not be able to use it anymore.

Decorators

In this section, we will discover the decorators and their use.

The name comes from the decorator design pattern designer (pattern decorator). A decorator can evade an object to change the behavior.

In Python, you may have already met, the decorators are identified with the character @.

The principle of Python decoration is to apply a decorator to a function, in order to return a new object (usually a function). We can therefore see the decorator as a function taking a function as a parameter, and returning a new function.

```
1 def decorator ( f ):    # decorator is a decorator
2     print ( f . __name__ )
3     return f
```

To apply a decorator, we precede the line of definition of the function to be decorated by a line including one @ and then the name of the decorator to apply, for example:

```
1 >>> @decorator
2 ... def addition ( a , b ):
3 ...     return a + b
4 ...
5 addition
```

This has the effect of replacing addition by the return of the decorator called function with addition as parameter, which is strictly equivalent to:

```
1 def addition ( a , b ):
2     return a + b
3
4 addition = decorator ( addition )
```

So we see that the decorator is applied at the time of the definition of the function, not during his calls. We use here a very simple decorator who returns the same function, but it could well be that it returns another, which would be for example created on the fly.

Let's say that we would like to modify our function `addition` to display the operands then the result, without touching the body of our function. We can make a decorator that will return a new function that loads the parameters, calls our original function, then displays the return and returns it (to maintain the original behavior).

Thus, our decorator becomes:

```
def print_decorator ( function ):
    def new_function ( a , b ): # New function
behaving like the function to be decorated
        print ( 'Addition of numbers {} and {}' .
format ( a , b ))
        ret = function ( a , b ) # Call the
original function
        print ( 'Return: {}' . format ( ret ))
        return ret
    return new_function # Do not forget to return
our new function
```

If we now apply this decorator to our addition function:

```
>>> @print_decorator
... def addition ( a , b ):
...     return a + b
...
>>> addition ( 1 , 2 )
Addition of numbers 1 and 2
Return : 3
3
```

But our decorator is here very specialized, it only works with functions taking two parameters, and will display "Addition" in all cases. We can modify it to make it more generic (remember `*args` and `**kwargs`).

```
def print_decorator ( function ):
    def new_function ( * args , ** kwargs ):
        print ( 'Call the function {} with args =
{} and kwargs = {}' . format (
```

```
5              function  .  __name__  ,     args  ,
  kwargs ))
7       ret  =  function ( * args ,  ** kwargs )
8       print ( 'Back: {}' . format ( ret ))
       return  ret
    return  new_function
```

I let you try it on different functions to realize its genericity.

Function definitions are not limited to a single decorator: it is possible to specify as many as you want, placing them one after the other.

```
1 @decorator
2 @print_decoration
3 def  useless ():
4     pass
```

The order in which they are specified is important, the previous code is equivalent to:

```
1 def  useless ():
2     pass
3 useless     =     decorator  (  print_decorator
  ( useless ))
```

We see that the decorators specified first are the ones that will be applied last.

I said above that decorators applied to functions. It is also valid for functions defined inside classes (methods, therefore). But finally know that decorators extend to class declarations.

```
1 @print_decorator
2 class  MyClass :
```

```
3        @decorator
4        def  method ( self ) :
5            pass
```

Although the definition is broader than that. The decorator is a callable taking a callable parameter, and can return any type of object.

Parametric decorators

We have seen how to apply a decorator to a function, however, we could want to set the behavior of this decorator. In our previous example (`print_decorator`), we display text before and after the function call. But what if we want to modify this text (to change the language, use another term than "function")?

We do not want to have to create a different decorator for every sentence imaginable. We would like to be able to pass our character strings to our decorator to ensure that they are displayed at the right time.

In fact, @ need not be followed by an object name, arguments can also be added using parentheses (as one would do for a call). But the behavior may seem strange to you at first.

For example, to use such a parameterized decorator:

```
1 @param_print_decorator ( 'call {} with args ({})
2 and kwargs ({})' ,   'ret = {}' )
3 def  test_func ( x ) :
4     return  x
```

We will have to have a *callable* `param_print_decorator` which, when it will be called, will return a decorator who can then be applied to our function. A parameterized decorator is thus a *callable* returning a simple decorator.

113

The code would `param_print_decorator` look like this:

```
1 def param_print_decorator ( before , after ):
2 # decorator set
3     def decorator ( function ): # Decorator
4         def new_function ( * args , ** kwargs ):
5 # Function that will replace our decorated
6 function
7             print ( before . format ( function .
8 __name__ , args , kwargs ))
9             ret = function ( * args , **kwargs )
            print ( after . format ( ret ))
            return ret
        return new_function
    return decorator
```

Wrap a function

A function is not just a piece of code with parameters. It is also a name (names, with those of the parameters), documentation (*docstring*), annotations, etc. When we decorate a function at the moment (in cases where we return a new one), we lose all this information.

An example for us to realize:

```
1 >>> def decorator ( f ):
2 ...     def decorated ( * args , ** kwargs ):
3 ...         return f ( * args , ** kwargs )
4 ...     return decorated
5 ...
6 >>> @decorator
7 ... def addition ( a : int , b : int ) ->
8 int :
9 ...         "This function adds the parameters` a`
10 and `b`"
11 ...     return a + b
12 ...
```

```
13 >>> help ( addition )
14 Help   on   the   function   decorated   in   module
    __main__ :

    decorated ( * args ,   ** kwargs )
```

So, what do we see? Not much. The name that appears is that of `decorated` , the parameters are `*args` and `**kwargs` (without annotations), and we have also lost our *docstring* . In other words, there is nothing left to understand what the function does.

Wrap functions

Earlier in this section, I talked about the module `functools`. It has not yet revealed to us all its mysteries.

Here we will focus on the functions `update_wrapper` and `wraps`. These functions will allow us to copy the information of a function to a new one.

`update_wrapper` first takes the function to add the information to and from which to draw it second. To resume our previous example, we would have to do:

```
1 import   functools
2
3 def   decorator ( f ) :
4     def   decorated ( * args ,   ** kwargs ) :
5         return   f ( * args ,   ** kwargs )
6     functools . update_wrappers ( decorated ,   f )
7 # We copy information from `f` to `decorated`
    return   decorated
```

But another function we will be much more useful because more concise, and recommended by the Python documentation

115

for this case. This is wraps, who returns a decorator when called with a function.

The function decorated by wraps will take the information of the function passed to the call of wraps. Thus, we will have only to precede all our functions decorated by @functools.wraps (fonction_a_decorer). In our example:

```
import functools

def decorator ( f ):
    @ functools.wraps ( f )
    def decorated ( * args , ** kwargs ):
        return f ( * args , ** kwargs )
    return decorated
```

You can now redefine the function addition, and test the call again help to see the differences.

TP: Positional arguments

We have seen with the signatures that there are *positional-only* parameters in Python , that is to say that can only receive positional arguments.

But there is currently no syntax to write a Python function with *positional-only* parameters . It is only possible, as we did in the previous TP, to retrieve the positional arguments with *args and to extract the values that interest us.

We will then develop a decorator to overcome this lack. This decorator will modify the signature of the received function to transform into *positional-only* its n first parameters. n will be a setting of the decorator.

Python allows us to redefine the signature of a function, assigning the new signature to its attribute __signature__. But this redefinition is only cosmetic (it appears for example in the help of the function). Here we want the change to have an effect.

We will therefore create a *wrapper* function, which will check the compliance of the arguments with the new signature.

We will divide the work into two parts:

- At first, we will perform a function to rewrite a signature;
- Then, in a second step, we will write the decorator's code.

Rewriting the signature

The first function, which we will call signature_set_positional, will receive as parameters a signature and a number n of parameters to pass in *positional-only* . The function will return a rewritten signature.

We will use the methods replace of signature and parameters, to change the positioning of the targeted parameters, and update the list of parameters of the signature.

The function will iterate on the n first parameters, to convert them to *positional-only* .

We will distinguish three cases:

- The parameter is already *positional-only* , so there is nothing to do;
- The parameter is *positional-or-keyword* , it can be transformed;
- The parameter is of another type, it can not be transformed, we will then raise an error.

Then a new signature will be created and returned with this new list of parameters.

```python
def signature_set_positional ( sig , n ):
    params = list ( sig . parameters . values
()) # List of parameters
    if len ( params ) < n :
        raise TypeError ( 'Signature does not
have enough parameters' )
    for i , param in zip ( range ( n ),
params ): # Iterate on the first n parameters
        if param. kind == param .
POSITIONAL_ONLY :
            continue
        elif param . kind == param .
POSITIONAL_OR_KEYWORD :
            params [ i ] = param . replace ( kind
= param . POSITIONAL_ONLY )
        else :
            raise TypeError ( '{} parameter can
not be converted to POSITIONAL_ONLY' . Format
( param . kind ))
    return sig .replace ( parameters = params )
```

Parametric decorator

Let's move on to positional_only our parameterized decorator. As a reminder, a set decorator is a function that returns a decorator. And a decorator is a function that receives a function and returns a function.

The decorator proper will be responsible for calculating the new signature and applying it to the decorated function. It will also create a *wrapper* for the function, which will check the correspondence of the arguments with the signature.

We will not forget to apply functools.wraps to our *wrapper* to retrieve the information of the initial function.

```python
import functools
import inspect

def positional_only ( n ):
    def decorator ( f ):
        sig        =        signature_set_positional
( inspected . Signature ( f )  n )
        @ functools.wraps ( f )
        def decorated ( * args ,  ** kwargs )
            bound  =  sig . bind ( * args ,  **
kwargs )
            return f ( * bound. args ,  ** bound .
kwargs )
        decorated . __signature__  =  sig
        return decorated
    return decorator
```

Let's see the use now.

```
>>> @positional_only ( 2 )
... def addition ( a ,  b ):
...     return a + b
...
most recent >>>  print ( inspect . Signature
( addition ))
( a ,  b ,  / )
>> >  addition ( 3 ,  5 )
8
>>> addition ( 3 ,  b = 5 )
Traceback (  call last ):
  File "<stdin>" , line 1 ,  in < Module >
TypeError : 'b' parameter is positional only ,
goal Was Passed as a keyword
```

119

```
1 >>>  @positional_only ( 1 )
2 ...  def addition ( a , b ):
3 ...      return a + b
4 ...
5 >>>  addition ( 3 , 5 )
6 8
7 >>>  addition ( 3 , b = 5 )
8 8
9 >>>  addition ( a = 3 , b = 5 )
10 Traceback ( most recent call last ):
11   File "<stdin>" , line 1 , in < Module >
12 TypeError : 'a' parameter is positional only ,
   goal Was Passed as a keyword
```

Classes and Objects

How to work with Classes and Objects in Python

Python comes with a multitude of built-in data types like, dict, list, set ... Have you ever thought about whether you can create your own data types? As a person, a car, universities, etc. It would be useful to create these types of data also for our developments, right? Well with Python it is possible, and that is where classes and objects come into play.

In this article, I will describe what is understood by a class and objects, and how we can work with them in Python.

Classes and Objects

As I mentioned earlier, classes and objects serve to create your own data type (that is, user-defined data types). A class is a type of data defined by the user, and the creation of instances of a class is related to the creation of objects of that type. Classes and objects are considered the main development blocks for Python, which is an object-oriented programming language.

How would we create a class in Python? The simplest class structure in Python would look like this:

```
class   ClassName   :          statements
```

As you can see, the definition of a class starts with the keyword class, and className would be the name of the class (identifier). Note that the name of the class follows the same rules as the variable names in Python, that is, they can only start with a letter or an underscore _, and can only contain letters, numbers or underscores. In addition, according to PEP 8 (Style Guide for Python programming), it is recommended that class names be capitalized.

Now we are going to define a class Person (person), that at the moment will not contain anything, except the declaration of pass. According to the Python documentation:

The pass statement does nothing. It can be used when a sentence is required syntactically but program does not require any action.

```
class   Person   :   pass
```

To create an instance (object) of this class, we will simply do the following:

```
jorge = Person ()
```

This means that we have created a new jorge object of the Person type. Note that to create an object we just have to write the name of the class, followed by parentheses.

We can identify what class Jorge is, and what space he occupies in memory by writing: print Jorge. In that case, you'll get something similar to:

```
<__main __. Person instance at 0x109a1cb48>
```

Attributes

The attributes are like properties that we want to add to the class (type). For example, for our Person class, we are going to add two attributes: name and school, such that:

```
class  Person  :          name  =  ' '          school  =  ' '
```

Now, let's create a new object of the Person type in more detail, completing these attributes that we just added:

```
jorge = Person () abder . name = 'Jorge' abder . school = 'Universit
y               o      f          l        i      f      e        '
```

Methods

The methods are how functions in Python, since they are defined with the keyword def and have the same format as the functions. In our class, we will define a method that prints the name (name) and the school (school) of a person (Person). The class will look like this:

```
class Person :        name = ' '        school = ' ' def print_name ( self ):
 print self . name def print_school ( self ): print self . school jo
rge = Person () jorge . name = 'Jorge' Jorge . school = 'University
of  life'  Jorge  .  print_name  ()  jorge  .  print_school  ()
```

I mentioned earlier that methods are like functions. However, the main difference is that the methods need to have an argument conveniently called self, which refers to the object of the method that is being called (ie jorge). Note that in a method call, we do not need to pass self as an argument, Python will take care of that for us.

If we do not put self as an argument in print_name (), Python will throw an error such that:

```
Traceback ( most recent call last ): File "test.py" , line 14 , in
    jorge . print_name () TypeError : print_name () takes no argument
s           (          1          g   i   v   e   n          )
```

Of course, you can pass more than one argument to the method. We are going to do the process of printing the name and school in one method, such that:

```
class Person :      name = ''      school = '' def print_information (
self , name , school ): print self . name print self . school jorge
= Person () jorge . name = 'Jorge' Jorge . school = 'University of l
ife' Jorge . print_information ( jorge . name , jorge



. school )
```

Test and run the program, have you obtained the same result as in the example above?

Initialization

In the previous section, we have initialized name and school, giving them an empty value. " But there is a more elegant way to initialize variables with their default values. The initializer is a special method, with name __init__ (the method is considered special and will be treated in a special way, that is why it has double underlines at the beginning and at the end).

We are going to modify the previous program to use the initializer. In this case, the program will look like this:

```
class Person : def __init__ ( self , n , s ): self . name = n self .
school = s def print_name ( self ): print self . name def print_sch
ool ( self ): print self . school jorge = Person ( 'Jorge' , 'Univer
s  i  t  y     o  f     l  i  f  e  '      )        J   o   r   g   e      .


p    r    i    n    t    _    n    a    m    e            (    )
jorge . print_school ()
```

Note that the initializer needs two arguments. For example, if we do not include the argument n in the initializer, we will get the following error:

```
Traceback ( most recent call last ): File "test.py" , line 12 , in <
  module >      jorge = Person ( 'Jorge' , 'University of life' ) Type
Error :  __init__ () takes exactly 2 arguments ( 3 given )
```

In short, with the classes you will be able to create your own data types, and with the objects you will be able to create instances of these types of data. Classes are also composed of attributes (properties) and methods that are actions that we perform on those attributes.

Python Math Library

The Python Math Library provides us access to some common math functions and constants in Python, which we can use throughout our code for more complex mathematical computations. The library is a built-in Python module, therefore you don't have to do any installation to use it. In this article, we will be showing example usage of the Python Math Library's most commonly used functions and constants.

Special Constants

The Python Math Library contains two important constants.

Pie

The first one is Pie (π), a very popular math constant. It denotes the ratio of circumference to diameter of a circle and it has a value of 3.141592653589793. To access it, we first import the Math Library as follows:

```
import math
```

We can then access this constant using `pi`:

```
math.pi
```

Output

```
3.141592653589793
```

You can use this constant to calculate the area or circumference of a circle. The following example demonstrates this:

```
import math


radius = 2

print('The area of a circle with a radius of 2 is:', math.pi * (radius ** 2))
```

Output

```
The area of a circle with a radius of 2 is: 12.566370614359172
```

We raised the value of the radius to a power of 2 then multiplied it by pie, per the area formula of πr^2.

Euler's Number

The Euler's number (e), which is the base of natural logarithm is also defined in the Math library. We can access it as follows:

```
math.e
```

Output

```
2.718281828459045
```

The following example demonstrates how to use the above constant:

```
import math
```

```
print((math.e + 6 / 2) * 4.32)
```

Output

```
24.702977498943074
```

Exponents and Logarithms

In this section, we will explore the Math library functions used to find different types of exponents and logarithms.

The exp() Function

The Python Math Library comes with the exp() function that we can use to calculate the power of e. For example, e^x, which means the exponential of x. The value of e is 2.718281828459045.

The method can be used with the following syntax:

```
math.exp(x)
```

The parameter x can be a positive or negative number. If x is not a number, the method will return an error. Let us demonstrate the usage of this method with the help of an example:

```python
import math



# Initializing values

an_int = 6

a_neg_int = -8

a_float = 2.00



# Pass the values to exp() method and print

print(math.exp(an_int))

print(math.exp(a_neg_int))

print(math.exp(a_float))
```

Output

```
403.4287934927351
```

```
0.00033546262790251185
```

```
7.38905609893065
```

We have declared three variables and assigned values with different numeric data types to them. We have then passed them to the exp() method to calculate their exponents.

We can also apply this method to inbuilt constants as demonstrated below:

```
import math
```

```
print(math.exp(math.e))
```

```
print(math.exp(math.pi))
```

Output

```
15.154262241479262
```

```
23.140692632779267
```

If you pass a non-numeric value to the method, it will generate an error, as demonstrated here:

```
import math
```

```
print(math.exp("20"))
```

Output

```
Traceback (most recent call last):

  File "C:/Users/admin/mathe.py", line 3, in <module>

    print (math.exp("20"))

TypeError: a float is required
```

A TypeError has been generated as shown in the above output.

The log() Function

This function returns the logarithm of the specified number. The natural logarithm is computed with respect to the base e. The following example demonstrates the usage of this function:

```
import math
```

```
print("math.log(10.43):", math.log(10.43))
```

```
print("math.log(20):", math.log(20))
```

```
print("math.log(math.pi):", math.log(math.pi))
```

In the script above, we have passed numeric values with different data types to the method. We have also calculated the natural logarithm of the pi constant. The output looks like this:

Output

```
math.log(10.43): 2.344686269012681
```

```
math.log(20): 2.995732273553991
```

```
math.log(math.pi): 1.1447298858494002
```

The log10() Function

This method returns the base-10 logarithm of the specified number. For example:

```python
import math


# Returns the log10 of 50

print("The log10 of 50 is:", math.log10(50))
```

Output

```
The log10 of 50 is: 1.6989700043360187
```

The log2() Function

This function calculates the logarithm of a number to base 2. For example:

```python
import math


# Returns the log2 of 16

print("The log2 of 16 is:", math.log2(16))
```

Output

```
The log2 of 16 is: 4.0
```

The log(x, y) Function

This function returns the logarithm of x with y being the base. For example:

```
import math
```

```
# Returns the log of 3,4
```

```
print("The log 3 with base 4 is:", math.log(3, 4))
```

Output

```
The log 3 with base 4 is: 0.6309297535714574
```

The log1p(x) Function

This function calculates the logarithm(1+x), as demonstrated here:

```
import math
```

```
print("Logarithm(1+x) value of 10 is:", math.log1p(10))
```

Output

```
Logarithm(1+x) value of 10 is: 2.3978952727983707
```

Arithmetic Functions

Arithmetic functions are used to represent numbers in various forms and perform mathematical operations on them. Some of the most common arithmetic functions are discussed below:

- ceil(): returns the ceiling value of the specified number.
- fabs(): returns the absolute value of the specified number.
- floor(): returns the floor value of the specified number.
- gcd(a, b): returns the greatest common divisor of a and b.
- fsum(iterable): returns the sum of all elements in an iterable object.
- expm1(): returns (e^x)-1.
- exp(x)-1: when the value of x is small, calculating exp(x)-1 may lead to a significant loss in precision. The expm1(x) can return the output in with full precision.

The following example demonstrates the use of the above functions:

```python
import math


num = -4.28

a = 14

b = 8

num_list = [10, 8.25, 75, 7.04, -86.23, -6.43, 8.4]

x = 1e-4 # A small value of x


print('The number is:', num)

print('The floor value is:', math.floor(num))

print('The ceiling value is:', math.ceil(num))

print('The absolute value is:', math.fabs(num))

print('The GCD of a and b is: ' + str(math.gcd(a, b)))

print('Sum of the list elements is: ' + str(math.fsum(num_list)))
```

```
print('e^x (using function exp()) is:', math.exp(x)-1)
```

```
print('e^x (using function expm1()) is:', math.expm1(x))
```

Output

```
The number is: -4.28
```

```
The floor value is: -5
```

```
The ceiling value is: -4
```

```
The absolute value is: 4.28
```

```
The GCD of a and b is: 2
```

```
Sum of the list elements is: 16.029999999999998
```

```
e^x (using function exp()) is: 0.0001000050001667141
```

```
e^x (using function expm1()) is: 0.00010000500016667084
```

Other math functions include the following:

- pow(): takes two float arguments and raises the first argument to the second argument and returns the result. For example, pow(2,2) is equivalent to 2**2.
- sqrt(): returns the square root of the specified number.

These methods can be used as demonstrated below:

Power:

```
math.pow(3, 4)
```

Output

```
81.0
```

Square Root:

```
math.sqrt(81)
```

Output

```
9.0
```

Trigonometric Functions

The Python Math module supports all the trigonometric functions. Some of them have been enlisted below:

- sin(a): Returns the sine of "a" in radians
- cos(a): Returns the cosine of "a" in radians
- tan(a): Returns the tangent of "a" in radians
- asin(a): Returns the inverse of sine. Also, there are "atan" and "acos".
- degrees(a): Converts an angle "a" from radian to degrees.
- radians(a): Converts angle "a" from degrees to radian.

Consider the following example:

```
import math
```

```
angle_In_Degrees = 62
```

```
angle_In_Radians = math.radians(angle_In_Degrees)
```

```
print('The value of the angle is:', angle_In_Radians)
```

```
print('sin(x) is:', math.sin(angle_In_Radians))
```

```
print('tan(x) is:', math.tan(angle_In_Radians))
```

```
print('cos(x) is:', math.cos(angle_In_Radians))
```

Output

```
The value of the angle is: 1.0821041362364843
```

```
sin(x) is: 0.8829475928589269
```

```
tan(x) is: 1.8807264653463318
```

```
cos(x) is: 0.46947156278589086
```

Note that we first converted the value of the angle from degrees to radians before performing the other operations.

Type Conversion

You can convert a number from one type to another. This process is known as "coercion". Python can internally convert a number from one type to another when an expression has values of mixed types. The following example demonstrates this:

```
3 + 5.1
```

Output

```
8.1
```

In the above example, the integer 3 has been coerced to 3.0, a float, for addition operation and the result is also a float.

However, it is sometimes necessary for you to explicitly coerce a number from one type to another in order to meet the requirements of a function parameter or an operator. This can be done using various Python's built-in functions. For example, to convert an integer to a float, we have to call the float() function as shown below:

```
a = 12
```

```
b = float(a)
```

```
print(b)
```

Output

```
12.0
```

The integer has been converted to a float. A float can be converted to an integer as follows:

```
a = 12.65
```

```
b = int(a)
```

```
print(b)
```

Output

```
12
```

The float has been converted to an integer by removing the fractional part and keeping the base number. Note that when you convert a value to an int in this way, it will be truncated rather than being rounded off.

Conclusion

The Python Math Library provides us with functions and constants that we can use to perform arithmetic and trigonometric operations in Python. The library comes installed in Python, hence you are not required to perform any additional installation in order to be able to use it.

Regular Expressions In Python

Have you ever wondered what is the key to *finding* a text string in a document, or being sure that a text *conforms* to some format, such as an email address, or other similar operations?

The key to these operations is regular expressions (regex) . Let's look at some definitions for regular expressions (regular expressions). In Wikipedia, a regex is defined as:

A sequence of characters that defines a search pattern, mainly used to find matches with and between strings, such as in "find and replace" operations. The concept was born in the 1950s when the American mathematician Stephen Kleene proposed a formal description for a regular language; they were commonly used in Unix systems in editors, in grep programs and in filters.

Another nice definition, is:

*A regular expression (regex or regexp for short) is a special string of text that defines a search pattern. You can think of regular expressions as wildcards. You are probably familiar with the wildcard notation like * .txt to search for all text files in the file manager. The equivalent regex is. * Txt $*

I know very well that the concept of regular expression may seem a little vague. Let's look at some examples to better clarify the concept.

Examples of Regular Expressions

In this section I will show you some examples of regex to help you understand them better.

Let's say you have this regex:

```
1    /abder/
```

This simply tells us to extract only the word `abder` .

And this regex?

```
1    /a[nr]t/
```

You can read the regex as follows: find in the text all the words whose first letter is `a` the last one is `t` , and between the first and the last one is present at least `n` o `r` . We extract the words `ant` e `art` .

At this point, I'll give you a little quiz. How would you write a regular expression that starts with `ca` and ends with at least one of the characters `tbr` ? This regex can be written as follows:

```
1    /ca[tbr]/
```

If you see a regex that starts with the circumflex accent symbol `^` , it means to find the strings that start with the values that follow the symbol `^` . So, if I used the previous regex, I would extract the strings starting with `This` .

```
1    /^This/
```

Therefore, in the following string:

```
1    My name is Abder
2    This is Abder
3    This is Tom
```

Based on the regex `/^This/` , the following strings would be found:

```
1    This is Abder
```

```
2    This is Tom
```

If we wanted to extract all the strings *ending* with some string? In this case we use the dollar character $. Here is an example:

```
1    Abder$
```

So, if we apply this regex to the previous string (consisting of three lines), we will get:

```
1    My name is Abder
```

```
2    This is Abder
```

Well, what do you think of this regex now?

```
1    ^[A-Z][a-z]
```

I know, at first glance it seems complicated, but let me continue and I'll guide you step by step.

We know what the circumflex accent is ^ . It means extracting all the strings that start with the given string. [A-Z] refers to all uppercase letters. So, if you read this part of the regex:, ^[A-Z] it tells us to find all the strings that start with a capital letter. The last part,, [a-z] means that after finding the strings starting with a capital letter, they must necessarily be followed by a letter from the lower case alphabet.

So which of the following strings will be found with the following regex? If you are not sure, you can use Python as shown in the next section to answer your question.

```
1    abder

     Abder
```

```
2   ABDER

3   ABder

4
```

Regular Expression is a really vast topic and these examples serve to hint at how and for what they are used.

A good reference to learn much more about regular expressions and see many examples is RexEgg.

Regular Expressions in Python

Now comes the fun part. We want to see how we work in Python with some of the previous regular expressions. The module for working with regular expressions in Python is re .

The first example was to find the word abder . In Python we can do this as follows:

```
1   import re

2   text = 'My name is Abder'

3   match_pattern = re.match(r'Abder', text)

4   print match_pattern
```

If you execute the script above in Python, you will get the following output None :!

The script works fine, but the problem is how the function works match (). If we return to the documentation of the module re , this is what the function does match () :

If zero or more characters at the beginning of the regular expression pattern string are found, it returns the object of the match found. Returns None if the pattern does not find the string; note that it is different from finding a zero-length string.

Yes, we can see that the function match () will return an object only if it finds the string of the pattern *at* the *beginning* of the string in which it is searched.

We can use the function search () , as we can find in the documentation:

Scan between strings to find the first occurrence of the regular expression pattern and return the object of the match found. Returns the None value if you do not find any occurrence of the pattern; note that it is different from finding a zero-length string at some point.

So, if we rewrite the previous script, using search () instead of match () , we will get the following output:

That is, the object will be returned match object.

If you want to return the result (string match), use the function group () . If you want to see all the items found, use group(0) . In this way:

```
print match_pattern.group(0)
```

It will return the following output: Abder .

If we take the second regex of the previous paragraph, that is /a[nr]t/ , it can be written in Python as follows:

```
1    import re
2    text = 'This is a black ant'
3    match_pattern = re.search(r'a[nr]t', text)
4    print match_pattern.group(0)
```

The output of this script is: `ant` .

Conclusion

The section is getting rather long and the topic of regular expressions in Python is a task that requires more than one source, if not many more sites and books.

This book, however, is a springboard into the world of regular expressions in Python making you have a broader understanding of this topic.

Data structures

Python Arrays

In this book, you'll learn about Python arrays, difference between arrays and lists, and how and when to use them with the help of examples.

In programming, an array is a collection of elements of the same type. Arrays are popular in most programming languages like Java, C/C++, JavaScript and so on. However, in Python, they are not that common. When people talk about Python arrays, more often than not, they are talking about Python lists. If you don't know what lists are, you should definitely check the earlier sections of this book.
That being said, array of numeric values are supported in Python by the array module.

142

Python Lists Vs Array Module as Arrays

We can treat lists as arrays. However, we cannot constrain the type of elements stored in a list. For example:

```
1.
2.  a = [1, 3.5, "Hello"]
```

If you create arrays using the array module, all elements of the array must be of the same numeric type.

```
import array as arr


a = arr.array('d', [1, 3.5, "Hello"])    // Error
```

How to create arrays?

As you might have guessed from the above example, we need to import array module to create arrays. For example:

```
1.
2.  import array as arr
3.  a = arr.array('d', [1.1, 3.5, 4.5])
4.  print(a)
```

Here, we created an array of float type. The letter 'd' is a type code. This determines the type of the array during creation.

Commonly used type codes:

Code	C Type	Python Type	Min bytes
'b'	signed char	int	1

Code	C Type	Python Type	Min bytes
'B'	unsigned char	int	1
'u'	Py_UNICODE	Unicode	2
'h'	signed short	int	2
'H'	unsigned short	int	2
'i'	signed int	int	2
'I'	unsigned int	int	2
'l'	signed long	int	4
'L'	unsigned long	int	4
'f'	float	float	4
'd'	double	float	8

We will not discuss about different C types in this article. We will use two type codes in this entire article: 'i' for integers and 'd' for floats. Note: The 'u' type code for Unicode characters is deprecated since version 3.3. Avoid using it when possible.

How to access array elements?

We use indices to access elements of an array:

```
1.
2.  import array as arr
3.  a = arr.array('i', [2, 4, 6, 8])
4.
5.  print("First element:", a[0])
6.  print("Second element:", a[1])
7.  print("Second last element:", a[-1])
```

Remember, the index starts from 0 (not 1) similar to lists.

How to slice arrays?

We can access a range of items in an array by using the slicing operator :.

```
1.
2.  import array as arr
3.
4.  numbers_list = [2, 5, 62, 5, 42, 52, 48, 5]
5.  numbers_array = arr.array('i', numbers_list)
6.
7.  print(numbers_array[2:5]) # 3rd to 5th
8.  print(numbers_array[:-5]) # beginning to 4th
9.  print(numbers_array[5:])  # 6th to end
10. print(numbers_array[:])   # beginning to end
```

When you run the program, the output will be:

```
array('i', [62, 5, 42])
array('i', [2, 5, 62])
array('i', [52, 48, 5])
array('i', [2, 5, 62, 5, 42, 52, 48, 5])
```

How to change or add elements?

Arrays are mutable; their elements can be changed in a similar way like lists.

```
1.
2.  import array as arr
3.
4.  numbers = arr.array('i', [1, 2, 3, 5, 7, 10])
5.
6.  # changing first element
7.  numbers[0] = 0
8.  print(numbers)      # Output: array('i', [0, 2, 3, 5, 7, 10])
9.
10. # changing 3rd to 5th element
11. numbers[2:5] = arr.array('i', [4, 6, 8])
12. print(numbers)      # Output: array('i', [0, 2, 4, 6, 8, 10])
```

We can add one item to a list using the append() method, or add several items using extend() method.

```
1.
2.  import array as arr
3.
4.  numbers = arr.array('i', [1, 2, 3])
5.
6.  numbers.append(4)
7.  print(numbers)      # Output: array('i', [1, 2, 3, 4])
8.
9.  # extend() appends iterable to the end of the array
10. numbers.extend([5, 6, 7])
11. print(numbers)      # Output: array('i', [1, 2, 3, 4, 5, 6,
    7])
```

We can concatenate two arrays using + operator.

```
1.
2.  import array as arr
3.
4.  odd = arr.array('i', [1, 3, 5])
5.  even = arr.array('i', [2, 4, 6])
6.
7.  numbers = arr.array('i')    # creating empty array of integer
8.  numbers = odd + even
```

```
 9.
10. print(numbers)
```

How to remove/delete elements?

We can delete one or more items from an array using Python's del statement.

```
 1.
 2. import array as arr
 3.
 4. number = arr.array('i', [1, 2, 3, 3, 4])
 5.
 6. del number[2] # removing third element
 7. print(number) # Output: array('i', [1, 2, 3, 4])
 8.
 9. del number # deleting entire array
10. print(number) # Error: array is not defined
```

We can use the remove() method to remove the given item, and pop() method to remove an item at the given index.

```
 1.
 2. import array as arr
 3.
 4. numbers = arr.array('i', [10, 11, 12, 12, 13])
 5.
 6. numbers.remove(12)
 7. print(numbers)    # Output: array('i', [10, 11, 12, 13])
 8.
 9. print(numbers.pop(2))    # Output: 12
10. print(numbers)    # Output: array('i', [10, 11, 13])
```

When to use arrays?

Lists are much more flexible than arrays. They can store elements of different data types including string. Also, lists are faster than arrays. And, if you need to do mathematical computation on arrays and matrices, you are much better off using something like NumPy library.

147

Unless you don't really need arrays (array module may be needed to interface with C code), don't use them.

Stacks And Queues In Python

Introduction

Data structures organize storage in computers so that we can efficiently access and change data. *Stacks* and *Queues* are some of the earliest data structures defined in computer science.

Simple to learn and easy to implement, their uses are common and you'll most likely find yourself incorporating them in your software for various tasks.

It's common for Stacks and Queues to be implemented with an Array or Linked List. We'll be relying on the `List` data structure to accommodate both Stacks and Queues.

How do they Work?

Stack

Stacks, like the name suggests, follow the **Last-in-First-Out** (LIFO) principle. As if stacking coins one on top of the other, the last coin we put on the top is the one that is the first to be removed from the stack later.

To implement a stack, therefore, we need two simple operations:

- push - adds an element to the top of the stack:

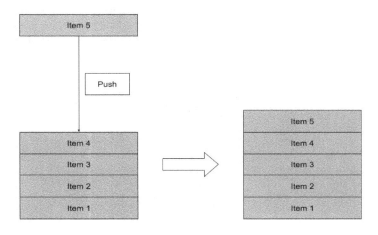

- pop - removes the element at the top of the stack:

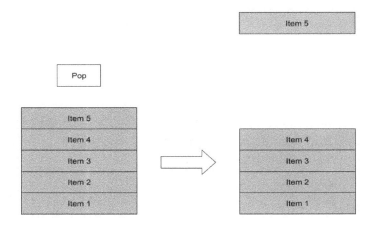

Queue

Queues, like the name suggests, follow the **First-in-First-Out** (FIFO) principle. As if waiting in a queue for the movie tickets, the first one to stand in line is the first one to buy a ticket and enjoy the movie.

To implement a queue, therefore, we need two simple operations:

- enqueue - adds an element to the end of the queue:

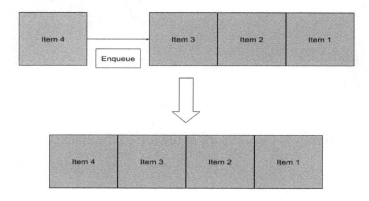

- dequeue - removes the element at the beginning of the queue:

Stacks and Queues using Lists

Python's built-in List data structure comes bundled with methods to simulate both *stack* and *queue* operations.

Let's consider a stack of letters:

```
letters = []
```

```python
# Let's push some letters into our list

letters.append('c')

letters.append('a')

letters.append('t')

letters.append('g')


# Now let's pop letters, we should get 'g'

last_item = letters.pop()

print(last_item)


# If we pop again we'll get 't'

last_item = letters.pop()

print(last_item)


# 'c' and 'a' remain

print(letters) # ['c', 'a']
```

We can use the same functions to implement a Queue. The pop function optionally takes the index of the item we want to retrieve as an argument.

So we can use pop with the first index of the list i.e. 0, to get queue-like behavior.

Consider a "queue" of fruits:

```
fruits = []
```

```
# Let's enqueue some fruits into our list
fruits.append('banana')
fruits.append('grapes')
fruits.append('mango')
fruits.append('orange')
```

```
# Now let's dequeue our fruits, we should get 'banana'
first_item = fruits.pop(0)
print(first_item)
```

```
# If we dequeue again we'll get 'grapes'
first_item = fruits.pop(0)
print(first_item)
```

```
# 'mango' and 'orange' remain
print(fruits) # ['c', 'a']
```

Again, here we use the append and pop operations of the list to simulate the core operations of a queue.

Stacks and Queues with the Deque Library

Python has a deque (pronounced 'deck') library that provides a sequence with efficient methods to work as a stack or a queue.

deque is short for *Double Ended Queue* - a generalized queue that can get the first or last element that's stored:

```python
from collections import deque
```

```python
# you can initialize a deque with a list
numbers = deque()
```

```python
# Use append like before to add elements
numbers.append(99)
numbers.append(15)
numbers.append(82)
numbers.append(50)
numbers.append(47)
```

```python
# You can pop like a stack
last_item = numbers.pop()
print(last_item) # 47
print(numbers) # deque([99, 15, 82, 50])
```

```
# You can dequeue like a queue

first_item = numbers.popleft()

print(first_item) # 99

print(numbers) # deque([15, 82, 50])
```

Stricter Implementations in Python

If your code needed a stack and you provide a List, there's nothing stopping a programmer from calling insert, remove or other list functions that will affect the order of your stack! This fundamentally ruins the point of defining a stack, as it no longer functions the way it should.

There are times when we'd like to ensure that only valid operations can be performed on our data.

We can create classes that only exposes the necessary methods for each data structure.

To do so, let's create a new file called stack_queue.py and define two classes:

```
# A simple class stack that only allows pop and push operations

class Stack:


    def __init__(self):

        self.stack = []
```

```python
    def pop(self):

        if len(self.stack) < 1:

            return None

        return self.stack.pop()


    def push(self, item):

        self.stack.append(item)


    def size(self):

        return len(self.stack)


# And a queue that only has enqueue and dequeue operations
class Queue:


    def __init__(self):

        self.queue = []


    def enqueue(self, item):

        self.queue.append(item)


    def dequeue(self):
```

155

```
        if len(self.queue) < 1:

            return None

        return self.queue.pop(0)


    def size(self):

        return len(self.queue)
```

The programmers using our Stack and Queue are now encouraged to use the methods provided to manipulate the data instead.

Examples

Imagine you're a developer working on a brand new word processor. You're tasked with creating an undo feature - allowing users to backtrack their actions till the beginning of the session.

A stack is an ideal fit for this scenario. We can record every action the user takes by pushing it to the stack. When the user wants to undo an action they'll pop it from the stack. We can quickly simulate the feature like this:

```
document_actions = Stack()



# The first enters the title of the document

document_actions.push('action: enter; text_id: 1; text: This is my favourite document')

# Next they center the text

document_actions.push('action: format; text_id: 1; alignment: center')
```

```
# As with most writers, the user is unhappy with the first draft and
undoes the center alignment
```

```
document_actions.pop()
```

```
# The title is better on the left with bold font
```

```
document_actions.push('action: format; text_id: 1; style: bold')
```

Queues have widespread uses in programming as well. Think of games like *Street Fighter* or *Super Smash Brothers*. Players in those games can perform special moves by pressing a combination of buttons. These button combinations can be stored in a queue.

Now imagine that you're a developer working on a new fighting game. In your game, every time a button is pressed, an input event is fired. A tester noticed that if buttons are pressed too quickly the game only processes the first one and special moves won't work!

You can fix that with a queue. We can enqueue all input events as they come in. This way it doesn't matter if input events come with little time between them, they'll all be stored and available for processing. When we're processing the moves we can dequeue them. A special move can be worked out like this:

```
input_queue = Queue()
```

```
# The player wants to get the upper hand so pressing the right combi
nation of buttons quickly
```

```
input_queue.enqueue('DOWN')
```

```
input_queue.enqueue('RIGHT')
```

```
input_queue.enqueue('B')
```

```
# Now we can process each item in the queue by dequeueing them

key_pressed = input_queue.dequeue() # 'DOWN'


# We'll probably change our player position

key_pressed = input_queue.dequeue() # 'RIGHT'


# We'll change the player's position again and keep track of a poten
tial special move to perform

key_pressed = input_queue.dequeue() # 'B'

# This can do the act, but the game's logic will know to do the spec
ial move
```

Conclusion

Stacks and queues are simple data structures that allow us to store and retrieve data sequentially. In a stack, the last item we enter is the first to come out. In a queue, the first item we enter is the first come out.

We can add items to a stack using the push operation and retrieve items using the pop operation. With queues, we add items using the enqueue operation and retrieve items using the dequeuer operation.

In Python, we can implement stacks and queues just by using the built-in List data structure. Python also has the deque library which can efficiently provide stack and queue operations in one object. Finally, we've made our stack and queue classes for tighter control of our data.

There are many real-world use cases for stacks and queues, understanding them allows us to solve many data storage problems in an easy and effective manner.

REASONS FOR LEARNING PYTHON

Why is Python growing so fast?

Python is used in a wide variety of fields, from web development to devops, but it has been increasing its use applied in machine learning and data science, which has accelerated the growth of Python . And its growing interest in the majority of programmers who are introducing themselves in these disciplines. Without forgetting the evolution that has had for web programmers or system admin the use of Python for years.

As a report recently mentioned, not only is Python growing but also many issues related to it. Thus we find the increase in the use of web frameworks such as Django and Flask or Pandas , NumPy and matplotlib for data science.

Using these tools, we can do much more than collecting and classifying information, creating scripts to automate processes, in addition to preparing a dashboard with that information.

Machine Learning by the hand of Python

The rise of Deep Learning with some frameworks like Tensor Flow has also motivated many developers to learn Python.

The exploratory nature of machine learning fits Python perfectly, so we can find libraries like Keras , PyBrain or scikit -learn to perform tasks of classifications, regression, clustering, preprocessing or generation of algorithm models.

As with the courses proposed to start with data science, in machine learning it is quite similar, although we can use Java or Scala, Python is still a dominant language in the academic field since it fits perfectly when implementing the bases of machine learning.

You can take a look at a large number of related courses in Coursera or Udacity in which will start with the Python basics.

Web development with Python

Well known we find Django , the free and open source web application framework written in Python. Nor is a newcomer and is used in production by companies with Instragram, Pinterest or The New York Times.

To this Python framework we can add some equally interesting as the minimalist Flask or Pyramid. In addition to these frameworks we can highlight the importance of creating Restful or GraphQL APIs with libraries like Graphene.

Python for Devops

The accessibility and flexibility of Python is also one of the reasons to prefer this language in DevOps. It's great for scripting and automating processes . The fact that tools such as Ansible and SaltStack are written in Python demonstrate the language's capabilities for automation and orchestration tasks.

In conclusion, should I learn Python?

Python is a great first language, as if it is your second, third or nth language . Its learning curve is less harsh than others, it has thousands of libraries that allow in a few lines of code to do what we set out to do. It allows you to evolve quickly, in addition to delving into more complex tasks, as you gain proficiency.

Obviously, recommending a programming language is complicated. It depends on many factors such as how you are going to use it. Nor is it the same to recommend a language to someone who is starting to program as another programmer with extensive experience in various programming languages.

As we said above: this is not a war of languages but due to the current momentum of Python you should be attentive, as it can be the language that will help you in your next project.

Looking at a Python Vs PHP From Another Angle

People often argue about which programming language is superior, PHP or Python. This is a hard and somewhat incorrect question to consider. So let's get a little more specific. Python is a general-purpose language. A lot of programmers don't simply use Python for web development alone. With the right set of frameworks, it can be easily utilized for GUI application development and more complex things. Tkinter and Kivy may help you develop an application for a mobile or desktop platform. There are also Python libraries that are being successfully used for Big Data Science and Machine Learning. Offshore development companies make some crazy things with this programming language.

PHP, on the other hand, is mostly associated with the web development. It's not like you couldn't make a non-web application in PHP. But you wouldn't.

So instead of doing a thankless job, we will try to decide what language is better to use for the web development specifically.

Let's talk numbers.

PHP was created in 1995 and since then has gathered an enormous community around itself. Programmers around the world still develop frameworks to expand the functionality of this language. PHP was used in the creation of websites like Wikipedia, Facebook, Yahoo and Tumblr. It undoubtedly dominates the web development market with its share of around 80 percent. So the question about which one is more popular, PHP or Python, for web development, is already resolved.

Python was created in 1991. There are much fewer Python-made websites, but this language wins in a traffic-per-website competition. It is used in Google services, YouTube, Dropbox, Instagram, Pinterest, Reddit, Spotify and Quora. It is also used a lot for the purposes of browser automation, machine learning, web scraping, data analysis and the Internet of Things.

If you plan on developing a website, you are probably going to choose between these two. Both have their advantages and disadvantages in certain situations, as many other programming languages. Both languages are open-source and multi-platform. They both also have a detailed documentation and an actively contributing community. But let's see how they differ from one another.

We already know that PHP is times more commonly used in the server-side web development than any other language. Its community has created many useful and popular frameworks for it: Laravel, Symfony, Zend, CodeIgniter, CakePHP and many more. With a decent knowledge and the right choice of frameworks, you can make the web functionality of PHP universal. Also, PHP syntax is quite forgiving, which some can assume a good thing. But I think it's important to have some standards in the code. Otherwise, it gets unclean and hard to read.

Web development with Python is more user-friendly. It has less web-dedicated frameworks but still, with Django, Flask and Pyramid, you can cover nearly anything regarding the web. If you prefer an asynchronous approach, there are frameworks like Twisted, Tornado, AsyncIO and AIOHTTP. You've got all the tools you need.

Also, this language has a much clearer syntax. It's strict but yet simple, highly readable and standardized. The resulting code in Python is always more elegant and transparent than the one in PHP. It will be easier to adjust and modify it later.

I guess there is no clear answer to our question. If you do want to dedicate yourself only to the web development and aren't afraid of any inconsistency in the syntax, you would probably consider choosing PHP. However, if you are new to the programming or haven't fully decided what would you do with the language you learn, try Python. With its easy learning curve and programming versatility, it is going to be a great way for you to start programming stuff.

Python Web Frameworks To Learn In 2019

Unlike other web programming languages, Python allows developers to create web applications with a concise, readable and easy to maintain code. By 2018, many web developers will prefer Python to other server-side scripting languages to accelerate the development of web applications and simplify the maintenance of web applications. But Python does not provide the built-in functions required to accelerate the development of custom web applications. Programmers use various Python web frameworks to write custom web applications in Python quickly and efficiently.

In 2018, web developers will have the option to choose from a wide range of Python frameworks. Some of these web frameworks are full-stack, while others are not full-stack. Likewise, some of these web frameworks receive updates frequently to complement the emerging trends of web application development. Depending on several factors, we believe that web developers will use these Python web frameworks extensively in 2018.

Django

Django is the most popular web framework for Python. Its popularity will remain intact in 2018. The high-level, full-stack web framework simplifies the development of large and complex web applications by providing a series of robust features. It is constantly developed to meet the latest trends in web application development. The features provided by Django further help developers to perform common web development tasks, such as content management, user authentication, RSS feeds and the site map. Django developers can take advantage of the integrated security features provided by Django to avoid SQL injection, cross-site scripts, cross-site request forgery and clickjacking. At the same time, Django helps programmers quickly scale the website to cope with the sudden increase in traffic. Here is a list of some of the best websites developed in Django.

TurboGears

TurboGears 2 is designed with features to overcome the shortcomings of several widely used web frameworks. The data-based web application framework is also written in Python. It allows developers to start building web applications with minimal configuration. TurboGears supports multiple databases and data exchange formats, along with the horizontal data partition. At the same time, it allows developers to simplify the development of custom web applications through the use of various JavaScript development tools. Users even have the option to use Pylons as a web server while taking advantage of SQLAlchemy and an ORM system.

Web2Py

The full source open source web framework is written in Python. Web2Pysimplifies the development of custom web applications by including useful batteries such as a web server, an SQL database and a web-based interface. It even allows programmers to create, modify, implement and manage web applications efficiently through web browsers. Users can even run Web2Py without problems in the main operating systems and web servers. They can even build web applications based on databases when working with several widely used relational database management systems. At the same time, Web2Py helps developers implement the MVC programming paradigm and prevent common security vulnerabilities.

CubicWeb

Web developers can use CubicWeb as a semantic web application framework for Python. In addition to following the common principles of object-oriented programming, CubicWeb further accelerates the development of custom web applications by providing reusable components called cubes. Developers can take advantage of the library of reusable components to perform common web development tasks efficiently. CubicWeb even allows programmers to use the RQL query language. CubicWeb has constantly evolved to facilitate the development of modern web applications.

Grok

The web framework for Python is developed based on the Zope Toolkit technology. Grok allows Python developers to accelerate the development of web applications by using the Zope Toolkit as a set of libraries. Developers even have the option to choose from a wide range of autonomous and community libraries according to the specific needs of the project. The component architectures used by Grok help Python developers simplify the development of custom web applications by leveraging content objects, views and the controller. Grok also provides the basic components needed to create custom web applications according to the various business requirements.

Zope

Zope is an open source web application server based on Python. Developers can extend Zope according to their precise needs through the Python code. Unlike other web frameworks, Zope is an object-oriented web application development platform. The features provided by Zope help programmers create custom web applications according to different business requirements. In addition, Zope supports both 2.x and 3.x versions of the Python programming language. Zope 4 also allows developers to take advantage of Chameleon-based page templates and improve the performance of the web application by reducing memory consumption.

Bottle

Bottle is a simple and lightweight web framework for Python. It is even distributed as a single file module, while leveraging the standard Python library. Developers can use Bottle to simplify the development of small and simple web applications by using features such as the built-in template engine, the HTTP development server and routing. Bottle also allows developers to work with several databases widely used through specific add-ons.

Flask

The micro web framework for Python is developed based on the Jinja 2 template language. Flask accelerated the development of web applications by providing an integrated debugger and development server. In addition, it supports secure cookies, integrated unit tests, sending RESTful requests and Jinja 2 templates. The developer can use specific extensions to extend Flask according to the specific needs of the project. Here is a comparative study between Django and Flask and how to choose the correct Python Framework.

Pyramid

Pyramid is a fast and lightweight web framework for Python. The features provided by Pyramid help developers create small web applications quickly. But developers can also use the Python web framework to convert small web applications into large web applications. In addition to handling web requests and responses efficiently, Pyramid also accelerates the development of custom web applications by providing features such as routing, view classes, templates, and static resources. Developers can even extend Pyramid without problems by integrating a variety of packages and add-ons. Here is a quick analysis of Pyramid vs. Django.

CherryPy

CherryPy is designed as a minimalist and object-oriented web framework for Python. Accelerates the development of web applications allowing developers to write concise codes based on principles of object-oriented programming. But developers can still simplify the development of custom web applications by leveraging the integrated tools provided by CherryPy for caching, sessions, authentication and static content. CherryPy even supports testing, profile creation and coverage natively.

In general, there are several Python web frameworks whose popularity will remain intact in 2018. But developers will still evaluate the pros and cons of each of these popular Python web frameworks according to the precise needs of individual projects. Therefore, the choice of the Python web framework will vary from one developer to another in 2018. Python developers can also use several Python interpreters such as PyPy for efficient programming.

HOW TO SHAPE YOUR FUTURE WITH DATA SCIENCE

The Scope of Data

Traditionally, we have seen data as something that tells what happened and it has helped us categorize the result of an event or action and evaluate whether we succeeded or not. It was like showing us the history in a detailed way. At the present time, however, since the technology is evolving at an immense rate, the combination of software engineering and statistics has enabled data to not just show us the past, but the future as well. This technique is known as Data Science, and it was introduced to the world after the term "Big Data" was coined.

Data Science is in its infant stage, but the rate at which it is taking over the industries and businesses, Glassdoor and Harvard are not wrong to call it as the best career of the future.

What are the Jobs of Data Scientists?

People who are the experts on dealing with the data and manipulate it in order to solve industrial problems are called Data Scientists. Their job includes the following points:

1. **Understanding the Problem and Collection of Data:** It is said that a problem is half-solved the moment it has been understood properly. For example, if a beverage company is looking to expand the business, Data Scientists have to understand the possible ways of expanding benefits. They have to collect Data about the company's resources, capital, targeted customers, demographics of people in which new shops have to be opened etc.

2. **Redefining of Data:** Many times the collected Data is not clear, or there are some missing points and disparities. It may seem like the end, but this is the beauty of Data Science. Data

Scientists have many tools which they use to predict the missing values and eliminate the anomalies. This process includes integration, cleansing, discovering hidden information etc.

3. **Transformation of Data:** After the Data has been redefined, it's the time to work on it and figure out some solution. Here, the Data Scientists modify and analyze the data to develop a model. This is actually the most important part of Data Science, and Machine Learning tools such as Python prove to be a great help.

4. **Displaying and Communicating the Data:** Once the model has been constructed, it has to be converted into a form which can be read and understood by others. Most often Data Scientists try to create more than one model so that they can be tested before deploying in industries. Most widely used tools for this purpose are Tableau, R etc.

Industrial Demand for Data Science

Today, the business environment is of setting trends i.e. foreseeing the future and becoming prepared for it, and since the Data Scientists are an expert of doing exactly that, their demand is only going to rise. Big industries such as E-commerce, Social Media, retail etc. are kind of devouring Data Science. But these are not the only ones since Aviation, Healthcare, Sports, Education, Public Administration, and Agriculture etc. have also understood that Data Science is the magic key to the future.

Data Science requires a deep knowledge of Machine Learning tools such as Python and R, and you also need extensive practice on many other tools such as Hadoop, SAS, Excel, Tableau, DataMiner etc.

How data science can change your future

What is data science?

At this time of big data, it is essential to have an efficient processing system for all stored information. Data science is part of this system and meets a growing demand from different sectors. Extraction of relevant information, pattern detection and statistical analysis are typical aspects of Data Scientist's work. With digitisation, all information about companies is becoming more vast than ever; this is creating a great demand for more logical and effective data management. These data are not structured, and the unstructured data grouped by organizations are of no use to them. A large part of Data Science is to organize that information in a useful way, by developing algorithms and Artificial intelligence to process the data.

What being a Data Scientist entails

To become a data scientist, it is important to have a good knowledge of business, mathematics and technology. Requires a combination of these. The ability to learn programming and logic languages will quickly be of great benefit to anyone interested in it.

For someone to obtain their certification, it is necessary to have some training in the domain. There are many well-known institution training programmes. They provide all the necessary skills and experience that will make a person on the path to being a full-time data scientist. Language coding will be part of any course, and also the different software programs used by professionals.

The courses provide connections with potential employers. This job placement assistance brings good data scientists closer to a new career with many opportunities to diversify.

Why data science is for you

With global growth in Data Science, there is much room for employment. There are many positions that are open to those who are certified in Data Science. Some of these are in the area of business analysis and software programming, but there are countless possibilities, varying from one company to another.

Part of the work is included in the specialized options in order to become a data analyst, engineer of machine learning, data engineer or even a scientist at data general, someone who can work in a wide range of tasks related to the data. These are all financially attractive positions. The remuneration can range from Rs. 8 to 15 lakhs per year for those who begin in this field, and more for those who have already acquired some experience.

For people who love to codify and appreciate a multidisciplinary approach, Data Science could be an excellent career choice. There are many ways to find solutions to a problem, and it focuses on finding the best for each situation. Combining programming with other technological skills is a good way for anyone with a strong analytical mind and logical understanding. It is the right path for you if you have some of these skills or if you want to learn them, in addition to the desire to join a rapidly growing field in which you can become an expert.

THE FUTURE IS NOW: MACHINE LEARNING HAS ARRIVED

Machine learning, a branch of artificial intelligence that gives computer systems the ability to automatically improve and learn from experience has been making serious waves for the last few years. More recently, though, the applications for smartphones and other small screen experiences have started to take shape, driving the way millions interact with their mobile devices.

Yes, Your Mobile Devices are Becoming Smarter

So what do these innovations means for your business? Machine learning can, essentially, make your smartphone "smarter" by improving a host of functions and processes instantly. In fact, most smartphones are already using some type of machine learning or intelligent automation application that aids mobile devices in becoming more efficient and effective. Predictive text messaging, for example, is one such application that's already become part of the mobile vernacular chances are, you use it daily without thinking twice.

As a whole, businesses are ramping up their machine learning investment, meaning we'll be seeing more of this technology, and more accessible versions of this technology in the coming months and years. For each generation, there's an added level of intuitiveness when it comes to mobile technology, your current smartphone is smarter than the computers that helped bring man to the moon, in many ways. From that end, how advanced will our mobile devices be in another 10 or 20 years? Smartphones could be paving the way for Robotic Process Automation (RPA) and evolving the very way many industries work.

What's Next for Mobile Machine Learning

Historically, machine learning requires a tremendous amount of power that mobile devices simply didn't have. However, businesses can now install special chips in drones, automobiles and smartphones enabling them to consume 90 percent less power. As a result, mobile devices, even without an internet connection can perform a variety of once-complex tasks, including:

- Voice Recognition

- Language Translation

- Virtual / Augmented Reality

- Smarter Camera Functionalities

- Improved Device Security

Going forward, envelope-pushers are driving towards even bigger, better, more sophisticated applications, think motion control and navigation, diagnosing and analyzing sensory data and more. Interactivity or perceptual interfaces are also capabilities that the new applications are expected to be equipped with, giving mobile devices seemingly endless capabilities.

Due to these unique benefits, machine learning on small devices is clearly becoming a priority for businesses. From intelligent mobile automation and RPA functions, it's all becoming a handheld reality putting the future in the palm of your hands.

Machine Learning Python: the language of the business of the future

Python has increased in notoriety in recent years and, today, could be considered one of the most popular programming languages in the world. The Machine Learning Python association has been favored by applications ranging from web development to the automation of scripts and processes. In fact, Python is quickly becoming the best choice among developers of artificial intelligence (AI), machine learning and Deep Learning projects.

Among the practical applications of this combination Machine Learning Python in the business world highlight the recommendations of Spotify or Netflix , it is also widely used by companies for their customer service, as it helps to promote self-service and improve workflows and the productivity of employees.

Why should every AI project include this language?

Before answering that question, we should delve into the difference between artificial intelligence (AI), machine learning and Deep Learning. In simple terms, it could be said that Deep learning is a subset of machine learning, and AI is the general category that contains machine learning.

AI is essentially any intelligence displayed by a machine that leads to an optimum or suboptimal solution, given a problem. Then, machine learning takes this a step further by using algorithms to analyze data and learn from them to make informed decisions.

Deep learning works in a similar way, but it has very different abilities; like drawing conclusions in a way that resembles human decision making. The result is a model that can learn multiple levels of representation that correspond to different levels of abstraction.

Today, Python is the developer's favorite language for a large number of applications. But what makes it particularly suitable for projects that involve AI?

The advantages of the Machine Learning Python combination are summarized in five:

1. **Wide selection of libraries and frameworks.** One of the aspects that makes Python such a popular option in general is its abundance of libraries and frameworks that facilitate coding and save development time.
2. Python is famous for its **concise and readable code**, and almost unrivaled in terms of ease of use and simplicity, especially for new developers. This has several advantages that make

Machine Learning Python an option to take into account since both machine learning and Deep Learning are based on extremely complex algorithms and multi-stage workflows , so the less you have to worry about developer by the complexities of coding, more can focus on finding solutions to problems and achieve project objectives.

3. **Agility.** Python's simple syntax means that it is also faster in development than many programming languages, and allows the developer to test algorithms quickly without having to implement them.

4. **Collaboration.** The easy-to-read Python code is of great value for collaborative coding, or when Deep Learning or Machine Learning Python projects change hands between development teams . This is particularly important in cases where the project contains a large amount of custom business logic or third-party components.

5. Python is an open source programming language and is backed by a **large amount of resources** and **high quality documentation**. It also has a large and active community of developers willing to provide advice and assistance in all stages of the development process.

Conclusion

Artificial intelligence is having a profound effect on the world we live in, with new applications that arise almost daily. Smart developers are choosing Python as their programming language for the multitude of benefits that make it particularly suitable for machine learning and Deep Learning projects.

Appreciation

We sincerely appreciate your purchase of our book that reveals useful information about everything you need to know about Python Programming Language. We hope you love it!

Thanks!

Leonard Smith.

www.ingramcontent.com/pod-product-compliance
Lightning Source LLC
Chambersburg PA
CBHW052145070326
40689CB00050B/2108